Transform Your Emotional
Reactions to Experience Personal
Empowerment and Well-being

LIVING A
TRIGGER-FREE
LIFE

BRIAN DESROCHES, PhD

ISBN Paperback: 979-8-9932030-0-3
ISBN Electronic: 979-8-9932030-1-0

Library of Congress Control Number: 2025920521

Publishing Consultant, PRESStinely: www.presstinely.com

Portions of this book are works of nonfiction. Certain names and identifying characteristics have been changed.

Printed in the United States of America.

Brian DesRoches, PhD
briandesroches.com

DISCLAIMER AND WARNING

This book is for educational and informational purposes only and is not intended as a substitute for professional medical, psychological, or psychiatric care. The information presented is based on the author's professional experience and understanding of neuroscience research, but individual results may vary.

Professional Support Strongly Recommended: The five-step process described in this book involves accessing unconscious emotional memories and may trigger intense emotional reactions, anxiety, or distress. The author strongly recommends working with a qualified mental health professional trained in experiential psychotherapies and familiar with implicit emotional learning and memory reconsolidation before attempting these techniques independently.

Not Suitable for All Conditions: This approach may not be appropriate for individuals with severe mental health conditions, personality disorders, active substance abuse, or those prone to emotional volatility or self-harm. If you have a history of trauma, PTSD, or other significant mental health concerns, please consult with a qualified professional before using the techniques described.

Medical Disclaimer: This book does not provide medical advice. If you are currently taking psychiatric medications or receiving mental health treatment, consult your healthcare provider before implementing any techniques from this book.

Case Study Notice: All client examples are composites created from multiple individuals with identifying details changed to protect confidentiality. Any resemblance to specific persons is coincidental.

Limitation of Liability: The author and publisher disclaim any liability for adverse effects resulting from the use or application of the information contained in this book.

Emergency Resources: If you experience thoughts of self-harm or suicide while reading this book, immediately contact emergency services (911), the National Suicide Prevention Lifeline (988), or your local crisis center.

Table of Contents

Acknowledgements and Appreciations 7

A Note from the Author 9

Introduction 11
    An Invitation

Chapter One 19
    What are Triggers? Shedding Light on 'the Feeling of What
        Will Happen'

Chapter Two 39
    How We Learn from Experience: Triggers and Emotional Learning

Chapter Three 61
    Emotional Learning: How We Acquire Knowledge About the
        Third Dimension of Our Human Experience

Chapter Four 75
    Recalling to Mind: How the Brain Remembers What We Don't
        Know We Learned

Chapter Five 87
    If This ... Then This ... : Your Predicting Brain Activates
        the Trigger

Chapter Six 101
    Our Shared Dilemma: When a Problem Is a Solution

Chapter Seven 117
    Optimizing Our Brain's Learning, Predicting, and Adapting
        Process: A 5-step Human Technology for Transformation

Chapter Eight 133
    Step One: Clarify the Problem and the Change You Want
        for Yourself

Chapter Nine..147
    Steps Two and Three: Discover, Clarify, and Validate the
       Threat Prediction and Your Protective Behavior

Chapter Ten...175
    Step Four: Identify and Clarify Prediction Correction
       Information and Experiences

Chapter Eleven...199
    Make Your Brain Right by Making It Wrong: A 5-step
       Human Technology for Enduring Transformation

Chapter Twelve..229
    Pattern Shifts: Navigating the "This Is a New Experience
       for Me and Others"

Chapter Thirteen...239
    Choosing a Path Less Travelled

Appendix..245

Resources...249

References..251

Bibliography...253

Meet The Author..255

Acknowledgements and Appreciations

I extend my deepest appreciation to Bruce Ecker, Sara Bridges, Laurel Hulley, and the late Robin Ticic and Paul Sibson. Words cannot express the profound influence you have had on my professional and personal life. I am grateful for your wisdom and insight, and the courage to share it.

To my many psychotherapy and coaching clients, I say thank you for your openness and willingness to follow a different path to growth and freedom.

Thank you to my friends and the guys in the St. Joe's Book Club. A specific thank you to Steve W. and Sheri K. Your encouragement and curiosity were often the grease I needed for the wheels of writing.

I want to acknowledge Kristen Kasza-Wise and Maira Pedreira of PRESStinely. Your patience and support were always there.

Finally, I want to thank my family. To my dear wife, Patti: Once again, your support, encouragement, patience, and belief in me and the message of this book have been essential to its writing. Kisâkihitin. And thank you to David, my son, and Christine, my daughter. Your inquiry about how it's going often kept me going.

A Note from the Author

All the examples in this book are based on real-life experiences and situations. However, stories from different individuals have been combined and integrated to provide more information while ensuring confidentiality. Additionally, details, names, and circumstances have been altered to maintain the confidentiality of all individuals involved. Any resemblance to a known person or situation is coincidental.

In addition to the examples provided in this book, you can access seven additional stories that focus on seven primary emotional learning themes I have documented since I started to write this book in 2018. Please go to www.briandesroches.com/trigger-free.

The five-step process presented in this book involves activities and processes that will create emotional discomfort and distress. Thus, you are advised to seek the support and assistance of professionals who are trained in experiential psychotherapeutic approaches and have a basic understanding of implicit emotional learning, the neuroscience of memory reconsolidation, and non-counteractive psychotherapeutic interventions.

Introduction

An Invitation

What if everything you've learned about overcoming or eliminating distressing emotional reactions and their associated problems is incomplete and out of date—or even mistaken?

This book invites you to be open to that possibility and to consider that:

- Understanding and managing your emotional reactions rarely leads to enduring change.
- Using calming techniques to soothe yourself after being triggered, albeit beneficial, does nothing to eliminate the trigger that causes the emotional reaction.

It is the same invitation I have been extending to my psychotherapy and coaching clients since late 2015.

What If There Is Another Way?

Drawing on recent breakthroughs in neuroscience and their practical application, this book presents a radically different approach. In doing so, *it invites you to walk a path of becoming trigger-free and experience a grounded sense of personal empowerment and emotional well-being.*

I could not have written this book without first accepting this invitation myself, an experience that marked both a profound personal and professional shift. Philosopher Thomas Kuhn described such a change as a "paradigm shift": a fundamental rethinking prompted by new insights. I want to tell you about that shift and why I wrote this book.

A Personal and Professional Paradigm Shift

Since its inception in the 1970s, the self-help psychology movement has been guided by a central message: if something is holding you back from the life, love, or success you want, take action to overcome or counteract it. Push through obstacles. Break down walls. Empower yourself. Achieve your dreams. Even now, those phrases stir something in me.

This *counteractive paradigm* encompasses various interventions, such as positive thinking, reprogramming beliefs, emotional regulation, improved communication, exercise, social connection, developing insight, and meditation, which form the foundation of most self-help books and therapeutic methods.

Until November 2015, I was fully immersed in this counteractive approach. As a psychotherapist with over 20 years of experience in private practice and a performance coach serving the dental profession, I was trained in numerous methods to help clients change behaviors, build insight, and manage symptoms.

One of my most effective tools was EMDR (Eye Movement Desensitization and Reprocessing). It helped many clients reduce emotional reactivity by processing **explicit memories of traumatic experiences** because they could be consciously recalled and narrated. EMDR helped the brain reprocess these experiences, diminishing their adverse effects.

But then came the many clients for whom EMDR was not suitable or effective.

They described childhood dynamics or early painful experiences, yet couldn't point to any specific trauma. Still, they suffered—sometimes with slight discomfort, sometimes with overwhelming emotional storms, bodily sensations, shame, or self-limiting anxiety. These patterns weren't rooted in conscious memory. They were coming from **emotional memories** stored in unconscious emotional memory systems, and there was no way to reprocess them.

For most of psychotherapy's history, these unconscious emotional memories were seen as unreachable, even permanent— "hardwired" into the emotional brain's deep, subcortical regions. Thus, the only option was to manage the symptoms they produced. That's why counteractive strategies became the norm: they helped us cope, not cure. Thus, relapses were understandable and even expected. I knew that from my experience of my seventeen years of psychotherapy and self-help work—when relapse happened, I blamed myself. I wasn't trying hard enough. I hadn't understood something. I just wasn't committed enough.

However, I now know that I was operating within the limits of the prevailing paradigm.

The Essence of the Paradigm Shift

At a 2015 workshop, I encountered a concept that completely reshaped both my professional and personal perspective: **emotional learning**. While I was familiar with terms like emotional intelligence, socio-emotional learning, and emotional memory, "emotional learning" was not part of my vocabulary.

Unlike learning we consciously pursue—such as mastering a skill or acquiring new information—emotional learning occurs **without our awareness**. We don't realize it is happening, and we certainly aren't aware of what we're learning. If you're feeling a mix of curiosity and confusion right now, you're not alone. I felt the same.

In addition, the term refers to both the process of emotional learning and the outcome, a form of memory called an **implicit emotional learning**. These memories—formed by emotionally charged events— don't store images, facts, or narratives. They are **patterns of associations between the experience of *what happened* and *how it felt*—especially**

during moments of intense painful emotions, such as fear, shame, loss, and danger.

Over time, these **implicit emotional learnings** can become **triggers,** even if we're unaware of the original experience.

When those triggers are activated, they cause the very emotional and behavioral responses that drive people to seek help.

But here's where the true paradigm shift occurred for me: I learned that recent breakthroughs in neuroscience had revealed a process that allows us to actually **update and eliminate** these problem-generating emotional learnings—not just manage the reactions they cause when they are activated.

Let me summarize this shift in five essential points:

1. **Emotional learning is unconscious and unintentional.** It occurs beneath awareness, without our consent or effort.

2. **Its outcomes—implicit emotional learnings—are stored as patterned emotional associations,** not as facts or thoughts. We experience them as emotions.

3. **When tied to intense emotional events**, these learnings can become triggers.

4. **Triggering these learnings activates the brain's protective system**, which responds with behaviors meant to prevent us from re-experiencing the original pain. Ironically, these "protective" behaviors become the very problems and symptoms we struggle with—anxiety, avoidance, anger, withdrawal, depression, etc.

5. **Thanks to 21st-century neuroscience**, we now understand how to **update** these emotional learnings, freeing us from needing and using the outdated protective behaviors they generate.

This shift—from counteracting problems to **engaging them** marks a departure from the 20th-century model of problem and symptom management toward a 21st-century model for **enduring transformation and healing.**

We're all familiar with revising what we've learned when we realize it's no longer accurate. The same principle can now be applied—through a specific process—to emotional learnings. When we update the learnings that once signaled danger, the brain no longer perceives a threat. As a result, it no longer needs to deploy the protective behaviors that may have once made sense at some point in our lives—but are now causing problems for us.

When I began to see these five principles unfold in my own life—and in the lives of my clients—I knew I could no longer employ the counteractive tools of the past. I had to integrate the new approach based on modern neuroscience.

Does this mean we should ignore our emotional reactions and problems? Absolutely not. Quite the opposite: we must learn to engage them. They're not flaws. They're clues—signposts pointing us to the deeper, unresolved emotional learnings that could now be updated. Trigger, be gone!

And no, we don't need to abandon all counteractive tools. We can enhance them with the foundational principles of this new paradigm.

Why I Wrote This Book

As I began integrating these five principles into my work, my clients started asking questions. I believe they, like me, were experiencing a paradigm shift—one that challenged everything they'd been taught about personal growth and change. Their curiosity inspired me to write a short, ten-page handout to answer the four most common questions:

1. What is emotional learning, and how does it create triggers?
2. How do these learnings disempower me and affect my overall well-being?

3. How can I uncover emotional learnings hidden within the problems I want to eliminate?
4. How can I update these emotional learnings once I become aware of them?

That small handout was the seed for this book.

In these pages, you'll discover how emotional learning shapes your brain's responses—and how a proven, neuroscience-informed **five-step process** can help you update and eliminate old, pain-based emotional learnings. While this is a self-help book written for a general audience, I hope it also contributes to the growing recognition of this transformative paradigm in the field of psychotherapy.

But there's a deeper reason I wrote this book.

Since the early 1990s, I've had the privilege of helping people grow, heal, and work to reconnect with their authentic selves. I've listened to stories of trauma, grief, anger, and longing. And beneath all that suffering, I've always heard the same deep desire: to be free from reactive emotional patterns that block joy, love, success, connection, and wholeness.

Before this shift, true and lasting change felt out of reach. But today, I know there's a way forward.

I know how to truly help others and, more importantly, how we can all help ourselves. When we walk in partnership with our brain's evolutionary bias for survival, healing becomes not only possible but sustainable.

This book is an invitation to choose that path—to become **trigger-free** and **experience personal empowerment and emotional well-being.**

A Final Invitation

In *Way of the Peaceful Warrior*, Dan Millman quotes a character named Socrates who says, ***"You have many habits that weaken you. The secret to*** *change is to focus all of your energy not on fighting the old, but on building the new."*

The old paradigm taught us to fight the old.

The new one? It invites us to build the new.

The word *"learning"* comes from the Old English *leornian*, meaning 'to acquire knowledge.' However, some of what we learned long ago happened outside our awareness, especially when it involved pain, fear, loss, or danger.

To truly transform, we must identify this outdated knowledge and **update it.**

We must **unlearn** what no longer serves us—and learn anew what sets us free.

We call ourselves *Homo sapiens*—the wise ones.

But wisdom alone is not enough.

This book invites you to go further and become a ***Homo leornian.***

Become a learning one.

Chapter One
What are Triggers?
Shedding Light on 'the Feeling of What Will Happen'

"You triggered me!" "That triggered me!" "I feel triggered." How often have you heard, said, or thought one of these phrases? Although the word 'trigger" is an old word—its origins date back to the 1660s and referred to a lever that releases a spring—its modern use has little to do with mechanisms such as levers and springs. Today, we associate it with painful or negative emotional reactions.

In this chapter, you'll:

- Learn where the word *trigger* came from and what it means today.
- See how painful experiences from earlier in life can turn into emotional triggers.
- Discover the ways we try to protect ourselves from the emotional pain embedded within those triggers.

A Brief History of 'Trigger'

The word "*trauma*" is the Greek term for 'wound'. The use of the word trigger and its association with trauma in human behavior and psychological research relates to studies of Post-traumatic Stress Disorder (PTSD) after World War I. At that time, it was known as "Shell Shock," "Battle Fatigue," or "Soldier's Heart," terms that referred to the activation of a traumatic memory causing a stress reaction. However, we don't need to have been in battle to suffer from a stress reaction.

We all have triggers associated with memories of minor 't' trauma. For example, being teased and bullied in grade school, publicly shamed by a teacher or others, or watching our parents have an intense argument. These experiences do not have the emotional intensity and threat level associated with PTSD or big 'T' trauma, such as being under attack in a war zone or physically assaulted. However, they can still have a significant adverse effect on our lives.

Yet how did the term trigger become so embedded in our everyday communication and culture? With the emergence of the Internet and online communication, the word 'trigger' and its various derivations took on a much broader meaning. It began to appear in blogs and social media postings that described distressing adverse emotional reactions associated with events, news stories, movies, social media posts, and interpersonal communication.

For example, I have been in many sessions with couples arguing about how they trigger each other, and individuals often tell me how a co-worker or boss triggered them. One of the most common outcomes that clients tell me they want help with is managing their triggers and reducing the stressful aftermath of being triggered.

Triggers and Their Adverse Effects on Our Lives

When we are triggered, our nervous system reacts in one of two ways: It may default to fight or push away mode—such as becoming argumentative or criticizing someone—or flee, withdraw from or avoid mode—such as walking away from a disagreement or placating someone to prevent a conflict—to protect us from reexperiencing the pain of a prior experience. Over time, these behaviors become patterns that are generated automatically. The past then controls our lives and futures, and we are not unaware of it!

You may have learned to recognize the emotions and physical reactions associated with your triggered states and perhaps identified what activates them. You may have also learned to counteract these reactions with interventions such as deep breathing, focusing on a pleasant experience, or reminding yourself that This, too, shall pass."

Perhaps you use exercise or meditation to help release and manage the distress of a triggered emotional state. As depicted in many television series, a shot of whiskey or a glass of wine may be the solution.

Avoiding actions, situations, or interactions that you know will trigger you, such as a restaurant where you used to go with your ex-partner or someone with whom you had an intense argument, is also a common strategy.

Maybe you communicate your triggered state to the person who you feel caused it, hoping they get the picture and stop doing whatever you think and feel triggers you. However, even if they comply with your request, the trigger still resides within your brain.

To illustrate how profoundly triggers can negatively impact our lives, I would like to share a personal story.

No More Mr. Nice Guy—Really?

I worked in hospital administration before I became a psychotherapist. Back then, I was stuck in a pattern of anxiety-driven go-along-to-get-along behavior—a hallmark of the Mr. Nice Guy syndrome. I had to avoid conflict at all costs.

This was evident in my relationship with Jason, the hospital's Finance Director. Monday morning administrative meetings were hell for me. Jason would take every opportunity to poke sarcastic jabs at me, like, *"When will you get the cafeteria to serve decent food? I ate better in the Army."* The room would erupt in laughter, including me, but internally, I was seething with anger and anxiety. Rather than confront him, I secretly entertained fantasies of revenge—imagining scenarios like slashing his tires or pouring water into his gas tank.

One day, a brochure arrived on my desk advertising a two-day assertiveness workshop. I seized on it as the perfect solution to my problem. Determined to transform from Mr. Nice Guy into Mr. Assertive Guy, I enthusiastically signed up—especially intrigued by the workshop's money-back guarantee.

The workshop was held over a weekend, and on Sunday evening, I diligently practiced my newfound assertiveness skills in front of the mirror. Over and over, I rehearsed my message: *"Jason, when you make sarcastic comments about me in front of others, I feel disrespected and angry. I want you to stop. If you have feedback, deliver it respectfully."* I practiced walking confidently, adopting a stern look, convinced I was prepared for Monday morning's showdown.

Monday arrived, and I waited anxiously outside the meeting room, heart pounding, legs weak, upper body tense—but ready. As Jason approached, something inside me froze. Despite my careful preparation, the only words I managed to utter were an awkward and anxious, "Good morning!" All my assertiveness drained away instantly.

The image of confidently standing up to Jason vanished, leaving me filled with disappointment and frustration. Once again, I reverted to Mr. Nice Guy, retreating into withdrawal and avoidance. All the effort spent over the weekend evaporated in mere seconds. Feeling defeated, I angrily criticized myself and channeled my frustration into an intense workout later that day. I wasn't even assertive enough to claim the workshop's money-back guarantee.

I now have a deeper understanding of this experience. Jason's behavior triggered an implicit emotional learning stored in my unconscious—an emotional learning that told me that speaking up for myself would lead to pain and suffering. Unaware of this at the time, my attempts at assertiveness were inevitably doomed. Recognizing this now, I feel compassion for the younger version of myself who struggled behind the protective facade of Mr. Nice Guy.

Triggers—Memories of an Emotional Learning

Every memory contains some learning. Think about a joyful birthday celebration—this memory is accompanied by an emotional association that links birthdays to feelings of happiness and fun. Similarly, memories of distressing events, such as being injured in a freeway accident, carry associations linking specific experiences (like freeway driving) to anxiety or pain. Later, when driving on the freeway, your brain anticipates the pain from that experience, creating anxiety in the present moment. If you're aware of the cause, you can often take steps to manage this discomfort.

However, most of our triggers arise from implicit emotional memories—memories that we are not consciously aware of, yet which strongly influence our emotions and behaviors. This is like experiencing anxiety every time you drive on a freeway but having no conscious memory of the accident. Without knowing the root cause, you can't address it directly—you can only try to manage or soothe the anxiety.

When your brain detects a pattern similar to a prior painful emotional learning experience, it automatically predicts a threat that feels imminent and real. This activates anxiety and triggers protective behaviors intended to shield you from re-experiencing past pain. All this happens even though the threat has its origins in the past.

Consider this scenario: Suppose you grew up in a family with an unspoken rule against talking about negative or uncomfortable feelings. Breaking this rule meant risking rejection or being ignored, as if you were invisible or didn't matter. Unconsciously, your brain linked the act of discussing unpleasant feelings with the intense emotional pain of rejection.

Now, years later, you're having a conversation with a close friend or romantic partner who begins sharing difficult emotions about a challenging day at work. Suddenly, anxiety rises within you. Although you genuinely want to be supportive and present, your brain rapidly recalls the implicit learning—speaking about uncomfortable feelings brings rejection and pain. Faster than you can say synapse, your nervous system kicks into fight-or-flight mode, causing tension, anxiety, or an urge to escape.

You might even recognize intellectually that your anxious reaction doesn't fit the present situation, yet the emotional memory remains untouched. Even if you explicitly identify your family's covert rule and explain it to your friend, your triggered reaction will persist because insight alone rarely changes implicit emotional learning. To remain engaged and present, you'd have to continuously override powerful, automatic emotional responses—a challenging, often exhausting task.

Here's an analogy to illustrate this inner experience of feeling blocked by internal sensations when trying to act freely or express yourself openly.

One Foot on the Gas, One on the Brake

Imagine getting into your car. You turn on the ignition, shift into drive, and gently press the gas pedal. Using the previous example, the gas pedal represents your desire to engage fully, listen closely, and be supportive of your friend. But suddenly, an uncomfortable feeling or sensation arises, causing you to instinctively press down on the brake pedal with your left foot. Although you're physically present, your emotional brakes have stopped you from truly showing up in the way you'd want to. Moreover, your right foot is still on the gas pedal!

Here's another scenario: You're attending a large dinner party when someone starts making critical comments about a close friend. You feel the strong impulse to speak up (foot on the gas), but anxiety grips you and prevents you from defending your friend (foot on the brake). Later, you might chastise yourself for staying silent. What happened? An implicit emotional memory was activated—a learned fear that speaking up will lead to pain. This mirrors my earlier experience with Jason; I wanted to assert myself (gas pedal), but my brain's protective action held me back (brake pedal).

Sometimes, however, the opposite occurs—you might find yourself unable to put on the brakes at all. In the dinner-party example, that could mean angrily snapping back to defend your friend, only to feel embarrassed about how harshly you responded later. That would be like me erupting in anger during the administrative meeting

As you might imagine, continually pressing both pedals (the gas and brake) puts strain on your internal engine, and driving without brakes entirely can lead to disastrous outcomes.

As I deepened my understanding of emotional learning, my patterns of reactive and maladaptive behaviors began to make sense. I finally understood why, despite years of psychotherapy, I'd struggled to make lasting changes. At best, I was managing my behaviors rather than resolving their root cause.

Psychotherapist Bruce Ecker, who introduced me to the concept of emotional learning during that pivotal workshop in 2015, explained it succinctly in *The International Journal of Neuropsychotherapy*:

*"Among the many types of learning and the many types of memory, the type responsible for the great majority of problems and symptoms that bring people to psychotherapy is implicit emotional learning—**especially the implicit learnings of vulnerabilities and sufferings that are urgent to avoid, and how to avoid them. These learnings form with no awareness of learning anything, and they form in the presence of strong emotion, which greatly enhances their power and durability.**"* (emphasis added)

Once I understood how much threat-associated emotional learnings affect our lives, I began to see my clients' experiences through a completely different lens. Rather than focusing on the problems and symptoms they wanted to eliminate, my priority in our work shifted to helping them uncover and update the emotional learnings that caused their problematic behaviors and emotions.

One of the challenges associated with this process is the paradoxical nature of emotional learning, specifically the anticipatory feeling of what will happen.

The Paradox of "The Feeling of What Will Happen"

Have you ever felt an ominous sense that stopped you from doing something you not only wanted to do, but knew would be helpful to others?

Imagine you're in a team meeting. You have thoughtful observations that could move the discussion forward, but a powerful feeling wells up, warning you not to speak. It tells you others will judge you as incompetent if you say what's on your mind. I call this internal sensation a *"feeling voice."* It's not a thought—it's a felt message. And it feels so true that you obey it, even when you don't want to.

Or maybe you've noticed a familiar pattern emerge when a romantic relationship starts to deepen. Part of you wants closeness while another part signals danger. A wave of dread moves in, and suddenly, pulling back feels not only right but necessary. You don't understand why; you just know you have to retreat.

Here's another scenario. Maybe your friends or family have told you that you tend to interrupt or dominate conversations with your "two cents." You've tried to change it, maybe even laughed it off, but the behavior feels automatic—as if it's just who you are. Eventually, you might withdraw to avoid saying something wrong, and then notice a subtle depression creeping in.

Or consider this: You have a good friend who never initiates plans— it's always up to you. You'd like to talk to her about it and believe she'd be open to the conversation. But when you even *think* about bringing it up, a tightness rises in your chest. Something feels threatening about the idea of speaking your truth. A "feeling voice" warns you: *Don't say anything— she'll be upset. She'll reject you.* So, once again, you stay quiet and pretend everything's okay.

These examples—and my earlier Mr. Nice Guy story—reveal two core features of emotional learning:

1. **When emotional learnings associated with pain are triggered, they generate anxiety and activate protective behaviors.**
   This process is *unconscious* and happens *fast.* You may find yourself scrambling for reasons—asking "Why do I feel like this?"—but all you're aware of is a compelling, hard-to-describe feeling that drives behavior you don't want.
2. **The "feeling voice" often dictates what you must do—like a command from within.**
   If we could ask someone in this moment to explain what that inner voice is saying, they might say something like, *"If I speak up, I'll be judged or rejected."* The message *feels true*—even when it doesn't make sense.

Take the meeting example: you want to contribute, but your feeling voice says, *"If I say something wrong, they'll think I'm stupid. I'll be judged. I'll feel humiliated."* You may not realize it, but your emotional brain has likely learned this somewhere—perhaps in school, at home, or in a previous work environment. And that old emotional learning now governs your behavior in the present.

Let me share a client story that illustrates this well.

Joan, a cosmetic dentist, was a member of two Dental Study Clubs. She came to me because presenting cases in front of colleagues triggered overwhelming anxiety—something she said she'd struggled with for as long as she could remember. Together, we uncovered the feeling voice that came up for her before presentations: *"If I make a mistake, they'll see me as incompetent. I'll be ridiculed."*

As we explored further, Joan recalled a memory from sixth grade. She had always excelled in math. One day, with visiting teachers observing, her teacher asked her to solve a complex math problem on the blackboard. She made a mistake. The teacher told her to sit down and said she could do better. Several students snickered.

When Joan reconnected with that moment, she felt a wave of shame flood her. "I know what happened 30 years ago is just a memory," she said. "But it feels like it's going to happen all over again when I present. I *know* that's not logical... but I still feel it." She also recognized the feeling of shame associated with memories of when other teachers and significant others told her the same message: You can do better.

There's a good reason for this. In the 1940s, Canadian neuropsychologist Donald Hebb coined a now-famous phrase: **"Neurons that fire together, wire together."**

Emotional learnings are formed during emotionally intense experiences. The stronger the firing or emotional charge, the stronger the wiring. These memories are also *state-dependent*—meaning the emotional state you were in when the memory formed becomes encoded within that memory network. Thus, the original emotional state is also reactivated when the memory and its associated learning are triggered.

This brings us to the paradox:

When we become consciously aware of and put words to the emotional learning embedded in a trigger, it will feel

like the truth—even when we *know* it isn't.

Joan captured this perfectly when she said, *"It just makes no sense that I would feel this way."*

That's the irrational logic of emotional learning. It's not based on what's currently happening—but on what your brain **learned to expect and thus predict will happen**. And that's what we'll explore more deeply in Chapter Five.

Protecting Us from What the Trigger *Predicts* Will Happen

You may not be one of the 34 million Americans who have sought therapy in recent years—or one of the millions who've spent billions on self-help books and courses, or life coaching. But if you've picked up this book and made it this far, something tells me you're looking for change. Perhaps you want to eliminate a problematic behavior, quiet self-critical thoughts, or reduce your strong reactions to what your partner or coworkers say. Maybe you yearn to connect more deeply with others, but something within you keeps drawing you back.

Whatever brought you to this point, I'd like to ask you a simple question: Have you experienced any of the following?

- Avoiding situations or people—even when part of you wants to engage.
- Saying or doing things in anger that hurt others or yourself.
- Feeling paralyzed by anxiety or weighed down by the heaviness of depression.
- Using substances to numb a vague but persistent inner discomfort.
- Losing yourself in codependence—focused on others while neglecting your own needs.

- Holding back professionally out of fear of speaking up or being wrong.
- Trying to listen better but feeling compelled to interrupt or insert your "two cents."
- Battling imposter syndrome or feeling that you're not enough.
- Playing the role of the People Pleaser or Mr. Nice Guy to avoid conflict or rejection.
- Repeating unhealthy relationship patterns with people who aren't right for you.
- Longing for intimacy but instinctively pulling away from it.
- Feeling disheartened after years of therapy that haven't led to real change.
- Getting trapped in harsh, self-critical thoughts that erode your self-worth.
- Knowing you're capable of more but holding back due to dread or anxiety.
- Struggling with a compulsive need to control or "fix" those you care about.
- Procrastinating on important tasks, despite your best intentions.
- Feeling drained by behaviors or thoughts that slowly chip away at your confidence.
- Struggling to maintain commitments—like an exercise routine or a healthy diet.
- Avoiding assertiveness for fear of disappointing others.
- Walking on eggshells around certain people or situations.

If any of these resonate, I want you to know two things:

- **First, you're not alone.** All of us—every single one of us—fall into these patterns from time to time. However, when they become our default patterns, they begin to subtly shape our lives in painful ways, affecting not only our well-being but also our relationships, health, and sense of self.
- **Second, these behaviors aren't character flaws or personal failures. They are your brain's way of protecting you.**

That second point might come as a surprise to you—or even a little disorienting. Many of my clients have had that reaction when they first realize it. These patterns they've been trying so hard to fix, avoid, or suppress are not signs of weakness—they are your brain's best attempt to protect you from emotional pain it once experienced, even if the threat of that pain no longer exists.

When you begin to see your reactions through this lens—not as faults, but as protective adaptations—it starts to make sense why deep and lasting change has been so hard to achieve.

And that's where your real transformation begins.

And the Real Problem Is...

By now, I hope a clearer picture is beginning to form. If you've been seeking deep, lasting change—fundamental transformation—for the emotional distress, reactive behaviors, or stubborn patterns that have been holding you back or causing problems in your relationships, then I understand your frustration. I've been there too.

For decades, the dominant approach has been to focus on *managing* our reactions or *avoiding* the situations that provoke them. We try to reduce the emotional pain that follows a triggering event, or we develop coping strategies to push through. But let's be open—this kind of change often feels like running in place.

Maybe you've stopped trying altogether. Perhaps you've accepted the adage, "People never change."

And maybe you don't even think of your experiences as being "triggered." You just know that a sudden feeling arises—a rush of emotion that seems to hijack your behavior. Perhaps the reaction is so automatic, you don't even notice it's happening. One moment you're calm; the next, you're withdrawing, lashing out, placating, or numbing out.

What you haven't known—until now—is this:

1. That your feeling and behavior are the result of a **triggered implicit emotional learning**—a memory your emotional brain formed long ago.

2. **Your reaction is not a character flaw or weakness.** It's your brain's natural **survival-biased response**, designed to shield you from suffering the pain encoded in that memory—even if the threat of pain no longer exists.

This explains why change has been so difficult. You've been trying to modify the *reaction* without addressing the *learning* that drives it. Insight may help. Temporary relief is possible. But true transformation remains out of reach if the original emotional learning remains intact.

No wonder so many people walk away from therapy or self-help books saying, "It didn't work."

So, does that mean we're stuck? Are we destined to keep reacting because of a painful experience hidden deep in our emotional brains—forever tethered to pain-based memories we can't even consciously access?

Are we up a creek without a paddle?

Absolutely not.

And in the next section, I'll tell you why I can say that.

A Transformational Solution to the Real Problem

If you had asked me those questions back in the 1990s, I would have said *yes*. At that time, neuroscience held that emotional learning created permanent, hardwired emotional memories in the brain—specifically, in its deep, subcortical regions. Once those implicit emotional memories were formed, they were thought to be fixed in place.

The best we could hope for was to work around them: understand our triggers, develop coping strategies, and, through effort and repetition, build new neural pathways that might override our old reactions. Thus, we saw the emergence of counteractive tools: positive thinking, daily affirmations, cognitive strategies, medications, mindfulness, and visualization techniques. Reprogramming the subconscious mind became a booming business.

Let me be clear—many of these interventions offer relief and can be helpful. But let's face it: they rarely lead to **deep, enduring transformation**. We were managing problems and symptoms, not eliminating their root causes.

Fast-forward to today, and I can now answer those same questions with a confident NO. Thanks to the application of advances in 21st-century neuroscience, we now understand that the emotional brain is not permanently wired by painful experiences. In 2007, Norman Doidge introduced the concept of the brain's neuroplasticity—the brain's ability to change its structure and function in response to experience and learning—to the non-professional audience. Scientists have now identified another natural, built-in process in the brain that can **unwire implicit emotional memories and learnings, allowing them to be updated and transformed,** taking advantage of its neuroplastic nature.

It's called **memory reconsolidation**.

This discovery has been a game-changer. For the first time, we have scientific evidence that shows how old, pain-infused emotional learnings— our deepest triggers—can be fully updated or even erased. This process is not about managing or avoiding triggers. It's about **transforming them at the source**.

We're just beginning to grasp the full implications of memory reconsolidation—for psychotherapy, personal growth, and anyone seeking real, lasting change.

And that's precisely what this book is here to help you do.

What Does This Mean for You?

You might be wondering: *What does all this talk about emotional learning and memory reconsolidation actually mean for me?*

Is this just another self-help framework wrapped in new language?

Is this book any different from the thousands of books on personal growth and emotional healing already out there?

Only you can answer that for yourself.

But what this book offers—and what I've seen time and again in my own life and the lives of my clients—is this: *When we begin to work with emotional learning and apply the science of memory reconsolidation through a clear, repeatable process, the results are profound and lasting.*

Here are just a few of the benefits people consistently report:

1. **More compassion and patience toward ourselves.**
   We begin to understand that our problems and symptoms are not personal flaws, but protective behaviors rooted in emotional learnings. This reframing softens harsh self-judgment and reduces the inner voice of self-blame.

2. **A growing sense of personal empowerment.**
   Practicing this approach gives us not only tools, but a new mindset—one that fosters real transformation, not just temporary relief.

3. **A shift from "Why am I like this?" to "What's happening now, and how can I change it?"**
   Instead of spiraling into harsh self-analysis, we develop a practical curiosity about how, when, where, and with whom we react. Each trigger becomes an opportunity for growth and strengthening our emotional well-being.

4. **Greater empathy for others.**
   When we recognize that others' emotional reactions are also protective behaviors born from their emotional learnings, we take things less personally. We respond with more curiosity and less judgment.

5. **Clarity in the moment.**
   As we begin to observe our triggered states more clearly, we come to recognize that the intense feeling of threat isn't happening now—it's a memory being reactivated. This insight enables us to respond with a curious intention rather than a survival reflex.

6. **A deepening sense of resilience and freedom.**
With each updated emotional learning, the distress of being triggered fades. What emerges is gratitude—for the calm, clarity, and confidence we begin to experience in everyday life.

How to Benefit from This Book

Although this book falls within the nonfiction self-help category, I don't see it as a typical self-help manual. If I could create a new category, I'd call it **self-informed, self-directed personal transformation.**

Yes, I could have written a much shorter book that outlined the five steps to living a trigger-free life. But I chose not to—because real change isn't just about having a formula. It's about understanding the foundation beneath it. That foundation is the neuroscience of emotional learning and memory reconsolidation.

For me, learning this information was a paradigm shift—a complete reframe of how I understood emotional reactions, behavior, and the healing process. I hope that it will be a similar shift for you.

Throughout the book, I've included exercises designed to support that shift—not just intellectually, but experientially. These practices are designed to help you integrate what you're learning and apply it in your daily life.

When you arrive at Part II and begin working with the five-step human technology for transformation, I encourage you to move through it with patience and trust. This process is grounded in evolution—it aligns with how your brain is naturally wired to adapt and survive. And while the brain may have a **survival bias**, it's one we can harness and optimize to help us do more than survive—we can use it to **thrive**.

An Important Caveat

As you move through Part I of this book, I encourage you to approach the material with an open mind and a healthy sense of curiosity. Take your time with the examples and stories. Pay attention to moments when you feel uncomfortable, resistant, or even strongly identified with what you're reading.

In either case—resistance or resonance—take note. Your brain may be offering clues about your implicit emotional learnings.

That said, I want to be clear about something important: The pain and suffering stored deep within the emotional brain can be intense. These emotional memories were encoded in high-stress or threatening situations, and the brain—true to its evolutionary design—has developed mechanisms to protect us from re-experiencing that pain. Even when the original threat is long gone, the threat-infused emotional learning remains in memory.

Although these protective mechanisms may have served us in the past, they are also the root of many of the distressing patterns and problems we face today.

Does that mean you can't use the five-step process independently?

Not at all.

Many of my clients have used it as a framework to create meaningful transformation in their lives. One client put it this way:

"I now understand behaviors that have haunted me for decades—especially the way I used to beat myself up. Just knowing what's happening has given me a kind of freedom I never thought possible. That alone has brought enormous relief. And I now know I can change what I learned."

The steps you'll learn are practical, grounded in neuroscience, and applicable to everyday life.

In addition to the six benefits I mentioned earlier, there's one more I often hear—summed up beautifully by a client who was learning to relate differently to his spouse:

"Once I saw and understood where her reaction was coming from, it helped me take it less personally. It was about something she learned— and it wasn't about me. I realized I could support her by not reacting. Because if I react, then it becomes about me and what I learned."

When you begin to see human behavior through the lens of emotional learning, you may start to free yourself not only from your protective patterns, but also from the feeling that you're the target of other people's reactivity.

Of course, the process isn't always easy. As you explore and uncover the emotional knowledge your brain has acquired—without your awareness—you may come across some painful material that is just hurtful to explore. If this happens, it is advisable to seek the support of a therapist. If you do seek professional guidance, I recommend working with someone who understands the neuroscience of emotional learning and memory reconsolidation. You'll find resources in the Appendix to help you get started.

Summary

Triggers are deeply encoded emotional learnings associated with past painful experiences that influence present behaviors and feelings. This chapter introduced the origins and effects of triggers and the transformative potential of understanding and updating them through the practical application of 21st-century neuroscience.

The Next Step

Now, let's explore what emotional learning is, how it affects our lives, and how we can become aware of and update emotional learnings that cause the problems and symptoms we all experience.

Chapter Two
How We Learn from Experience:

Triggers and Emotional Learning

What does the phrase *'learning from experience'* mean to you? For Albert Einstein, it meant, *"The only source of knowledge is experience."* For Julius Caesar, it meant, *'Experience is the teacher of all things."* While we often use the phrase casually, its meaning runs deeper—especially when it comes to understanding how our emotions shape our lives. Experience and learning are closely related. However, rather than assuming we share a common understanding of that relationship, I want to clarify what I mean.

The word *"experience"* comes from the Latin *experiri,* meaning 'out of what one goes through,' and *learning,* as I mentioned in the Introduction, refers to the acquisition of knowledge. Thus, **learning from experience is the acquisition of knowledge as an outcome of what we go through—moment by moment, interaction by interaction—as we move through life.**

This chapter will explore specific aspects of this process:

- The **three categories of learning** that are associated with the **three dimensions of human experience.**
- The difference between **intentional** and **unintentional** learning.
- How these ideas create the foundation for understanding **emotional learning**—the unconscious, experience-based process by which our emotional brain learns to associate feelings with people, interactions, situations, and events.

Let's start by examining three different categories of learning and how they correspond to human experience.

Three Dimensions of Human Experience and Three Categories of Learning

It is a fact with which we are all familiar: *All learning has the potential to become a consolidated neural network of information that we call a memory,* as depicted in Illustration 2.1.

Illustration 2.1 – Learning from Experience Becomes a Memory

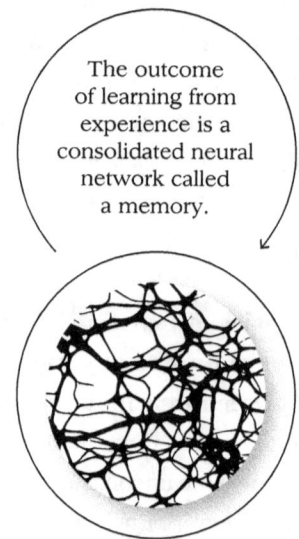

The outcome of learning from experience is a consolidated neural network called a memory.

What most of us don't know is that there are three categories of learning that correspond to the three dimensions of the human experience as depicted in Illustration 2.2 and described in the paragraphs that follow it.

Illustration 2.2 – Three Dimensions of the Human Experience and Three Categories of Memory and Learning

THREE DIMENSIONS
OF HUMAN
EXPERIENCE

THREE CATEGORIES
OF MEMORY AND
LEARNING

Dimension One
The physical world
and visible human
behavior.

Category One
Skills and
manual tasks.

Dimension Two
The internal
experience of
thoughts, stories,
beliefs, knowledge,
and mental activities.

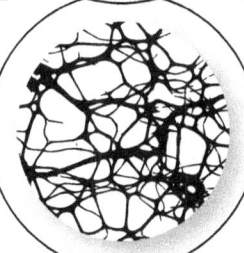

Category Two
Facts, information,
mental processes.

Dimension Three
The internal
experience of
emotions, feelings,
and physical
sensations.

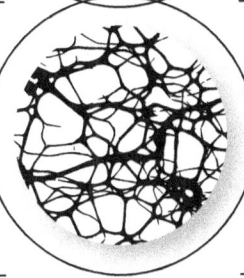

Category Three
Emotions,feelings, and
physical sensations
associated with
people, interactions,
situations, and events.

Dimension One and Category One – Skills and Manual Tasks

The first category of memory and learning involves acquiring knowledge to perform the observable manual skills necessary for daily living, our careers, and recreational pursuits. These can be as simple as typing on a keyboard or as complex as driving a car. Think about the hundreds of actions that you perform as you move through your day: knowing how to brush your teeth, prepare a meal, do the work required by your job, communicate with others, and participate in recreational pursuits such as skiing, tennis, or golf. You must have acquired the knowledge to do these actions at some point.

Dimension Two and Category Two – Facts, Information, and Mental Processes

The second category is associated with information, facts, and mental processes. Although this category cannot be observed directly, the outcomes of applying this knowledge usually can. For example, I could not have written this book without learning grammar and how to construct a sentence. You could watch me type a sentence, but you wouldn't see the mental processes I've learned and am using to create sentences. Whatever your chosen profession, you must have acquired the knowledge base that enables you to perform the mental processes that your job requires. As with the first category, our daily lives depend upon knowing and using information, facts, and processes.

Dimension Three and Category Three – Emotions, Feelings, and Physical Sensations Associated with People, Interactions, Situations, and Events

This book is about this third category of learning—the process by which *our emotional brains learn to associate specific feelings with specific experiences*—especially in moments involving pain, fear, threat, safety, loss, connection, or reward. This learning occurs early in life, especially during the first fifteen years, and typically happens *without our awareness*.

If you were to search the term "emotional learning" online, you'd find millions of results, mainly related to emotional regulation, emotional intelligence, or social-emotional learning in schools. Emotional learning does not fit into any of these topic areas. We do not teach it in our educational systems, and it is seldom, if ever, part of our daily conversations.

To make this learning process more concrete, let's examine how the three categories of learning can be illustrated in a single activity, such as playing Pickleball.

Illustration 2.3 – Three Categories of Memory and Learning Associated with Pickleball

THREE DIMENSIONS OF HUMAN EXPERIENCE

THREE CATEGORIES OF MEMORY AND LEARNING ABOUT PLAYING PICKLEBALL

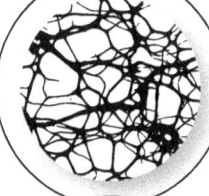

Dimension One
The physical world and visible human behavior.

Category One
To play Pickleball, you need to learn basic Pickleball skills.

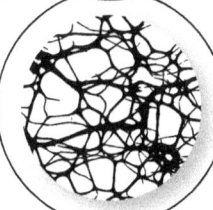

Dimension Two
The internal experience of thoughts, stories, beliefs, and mental activities.

Category Two
You also need to learn the rules of the game.

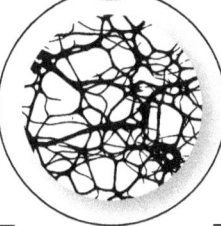

Dimension Three
The internal experience of emotions, feelings, and physical sensations.

Category Three
Pickleball can be fun and a social experience, and frustrating as you develop your skills.

Let's say you've recently taken up the game. At first, you had to learn the manual skills: how to hold the paddle, serve the ball, move your feet, return shots, etc. You also had to learn the rules of the game and mental strategies—things like where to place the ball, how to anticipate your opponent's moves, and when to stay back or approach the net.

These are the first two categories of learning:

- **Manual/behavioral** (your physical technique)
- **Cognitive/informational** (your knowledge of the game and strategies)

Now, let's say you've been enjoying friendly games with friends. But one day, someone new joins the group—a highly competitive player who takes the game way too seriously. He argues over line calls, keeps score aggressively, and injects tension into the match. It's uncomfortable. You leave that day with a knot in your stomach, even though your skills and knowledge haven't changed.

Without meaning to, your emotional brain just formed a new association:

Playing with someone who has to win is unpleasant and generates distress.

The next time your friends invite you to play, you casually ask, *"Is that guy coming again?"* When they say maybe, you feel that same pinch in your stomach. That physical sensation is the result of a **triggered emotional learning**—a feeling-memory linked to a previous unpleasant experience.

This is the third category of learning:

- **Emotional learning** (your emotional brain's patterned association of fun and frustration playing the game and the discomfort with the aggressive player).

You didn't set out to learn that competitive Pickleball players make you anxious. However, your emotional brain took that experience and turned it into an emotional memory and a learning experience. So now, when you think about that person, your body reacts. You hesitate. You second-guess yourself. You brace for impact.

That's emotional learning at work.

Intentional Learning

At the age of 87, just months before his death, Michelangelo reportedly said, *"I am still learning."*

This kind of learning is intentional. It's the kind we pursue consciously—with effort, focus, and curiosity. We read books, take courses, watch videos, practice skills, or reflect on past learnings with the goal of growth and improvement.

Take a moment to reflect on some intentional learning experiences that have shaped your life. Remember the subjects in school that you were determined to master and those that didn't quite spark your interest. Consider your deliberate decisions when choosing a career and the education required for success. These were all instances of intentional learning, where you took control of your learning journey. Think about the intentional learning involved with your recreational pursuits and hobbies.

This is the kind of learning we are familiar with. When something sparks our interest, we become motivated to learn and take steps to acquire new knowledge or update what we already know.

Although this book discusses intentional learning, it's about something more powerful—and more elusive.

It's about **unintentional learning**: the kind that happens without your awareness, without your permission, and without your conscious knowing of what was learned. That's what makes **emotional learning** so impactful:

- It bypasses logic.
- It doesn't ask for your approval.
- It simply associates this ... (a person, interaction, situation, or event) with that ... (emotions and feelings) and records it as a pattern in your brain.

In the Introduction, I mentioned a workshop I attended in 2015 that changed everything for me. That workshop didn't just give me information—it revealed a process that helped me uncover one of my unintentional emotional learnings. It was a learning that had blocked me for over a decade, and I didn't even know it existed.

Let me tell you that story.

A Story about Unintentional Learning

In the 1990s, two of my books were published by major New York publishing houses:

- *Reclaiming Your Self* explored the four stages of recovery from codependence.
- *Your Boss Is Not Your Mother* offered insights into emotional dynamics in the workplace and was translated into five foreign languages—including Chinese.

By the mid-2000s, I was ready to write again. I had ideas. I had experience. I had two published books under my belt. On the outside, I had every reason to feel confident.

But every time I sat down to write—or even *thought* about writing—I felt anxious. Not just distracted or uninspired. I mean full-body distress. Tightness. Dread. Inner chaos.

Weeks turned into months, and months turned into years.

This wasn't casual procrastination. It was what is commonly called **toxic procrastination**—a frustrating, all-consuming avoidance that led to harsh self-judgment, anxiety, and endless loops of internal criticism: "*Why can't I just do this?*"

Like many people caught in self-defeating patterns, I had *reasons*. I was busy with clients. I had a family life, and I had research to do. Maybe I just needed the right environment, the right tool, the right time.

I tried everything: a new laptop; dictation software; a deep cobalt blue pen; writing retreats; a writing coach; prayer, meditation, and even more therapy.

Still, I was stuck.

And every day I wasn't writing, a critical feeling voice got louder: *"What the f&'%k is wrong with me?"*

Then in 2015, I attended a workshop led by the Coherence Psychology Institute. I didn't go there expecting to free myself from procrastination. But that's precisely what happened. And it happened not because I learned a new writing strategy. I uncovered a pain-infused emotional learning I didn't know I had acquired.

Let me explain.

How Emotional Learning Fueled My Toxic Procrastination

When I submitted the manuscript for *Your Boss Is Not Your Mother,* my publisher responded with enthusiasm about the content—but also requested a complete rewrite in a different format.

They felt the ideas were strong, but the structure and style needed a fresh approach. I agreed. Their reasoning made sense, and I was open to collaboration. A professional writer was brought in, and we refined the manuscript.

On the surface, I accepted the process.

But emotionally, something very different was happening.

Despite their praise, my emotional brain absorbed a very different feeling message that associated writing with shame and rejection—one I wasn't consciously aware of:

- *I'm not good enough.*
- *I'm a failure.*
- *I'm a fraud pretending to be a writer.*

These feelings weren't logical. They didn't reflect what the publisher or agent intended. But that didn't matter. Deep down, my emotional brain learned something about writing that I didn't know it learned. Like all emotional learnings, this one was a **felt association**, not a thought.

So, years later, when I attempted to write again, my brain recalled what it had learned about writing—from its perspective, writing was a threat to my survival.

That unconscious learning created a kind of neural scar tissue that triggered anxiety any time I even considered writing again, and here's the thing: I didn't know any of this at the time. All I knew was that I couldn't write, and I had no idea why.

Later, I would come to understand that the emotional learning I acquired from that publishing experience had roots that went even deeper—to unresolved emotional learnings of shame from growing up with an alcoholic father. Just as I pretended as a child that all was well with my family, I also felt like people would see that I was a fraud, someone pretending to be a writer. But I didn't know that.

The thought of writing again stirred me up, and it was an uncomfortable, anxious stirring.

Being Stirred Up

The word *"emotion"* comes from the Middle French word émouvoir, meaning 'to stir up.'

That's what emotions do: They stir us up; they activate us; they cause us to take action, either internally or externally.

There are four core facts about how emotions shape our behavior:

1. **Emotions stir us up.**
2. **Emotions can be painful or pleasurable.**

3. We invite, move towards, and seek people, interactions, situations, and activities that generate positive and pleasurable emotions.

4. We push away, withdraw from, and avoid people, interactions, situations, and activities that generate negative and painful emotions.

Fact #3 is evident to all of us. Think about an activity that you enjoy doing. It may be hiking in the woods, playing tennis with friends, or reading a good novel. While you may identify with the activity itself, what you're drawn to is the *emotional experience* your brain has associated with it.

The same principle works in reverse.

When we avoid something, we're usually not avoiding the activity itself—we're avoiding the *emotion* our brain has learned to associate with it.

Robert and the Fear of Recreational Sports

Robert wanted to join a city soccer league but kept hesitating. He said, "I'm just a klutz when it comes to sports." However, that wasn't the whole story.

As we explored further, Robert recalled his all-boys high school, where being bad at sports came with cruel labels—wussy, klutz, weak. He wasn't just remembering words; he was remembering the shame that came with them.

His emotional brain had learned to associate athletic participation with humiliation and rejection. Years later, even though no one was mocking him, the feeling returned any time he thought about playing sports.

Let's look at a few more simple examples of how emotional learning shapes behavior—not through conscious choice, but through unconscious emotional associations.

Public Speaking

Let's say you avoid public speaking. It's not the act of standing at a podium that your brain resists—it's the emotional memory possibly tied to painful experiences of embarrassment, shame, or being judged. If you grew up being mocked for speaking out, those associations get stored. And even if you're now capable and articulate, your brain still recognizes the same pain-infused emotional learning when you try to speak in public.

Avoiding Conflict

Many people dislike conflict, but some go to great lengths to avoid even the slightest disagreement—often at the expense of their needs or self-respect.

When someone has learned—often in childhood—that conflict leads to distress, punishment, or rejection, their brain stores that patterned association. Thus, in adulthood, the prospect of a simple disagreement can feel dangerous.

Saying Yes When You Want to Say No

Maybe you struggle to say no. You overcommit. You take care of others at your own expense. Why? Sometimes, the emotional brain has learned that saying no leads to the pain of rejection. Maybe when you said no to our parents, you were scolded and told that when children say no to their parents, they hurt God and will go to Hell. Once again, the emotional brain learned that saying no resulted in painful feelings.

Struggling to Accept Compliments

Compliments are meant to be uplifting. But for some people, they're deeply uncomfortable.

If you were raised in a family where accepting praise was frowned upon—or where humility was taken to the extreme—you may have learned that acknowledging compliments is dangerous. So, when someone praises you, you tend to deflect. You brush it off. You feel awkward.

The moment may seem insignificant, but the emotional memory it evokes can run deep.

When We Don't Know What We've Learned

Even when we know what we withdraw from or avoid, we're usually unaware of *why* those reactions are so strong. Emotional learning, as I've mentioned, is unconscious. We don't know what our emotional brain has learned—we just know how we feel.

Before I understood this process, all I knew was that I was procrastinating and couldn't write. It made no sense. I had no access to the emotional learning that was shaping my behavior.

This is how it often works. You get triggered and react. You analyze, problem-solve, blame yourself—but the real cause remains hidden.

Let me share two stories that illustrate this process in action.

Ashley's Anxious ABCs

Do you know anyone who becomes anxious while teaching the alphabet? I imagine very few. Ashley was my first introduction to the anxious ABCs.

She came to me wanting to work on performance anxiety. But before we started, she said, *"There's something else that's really bothering me."* Her voice grew quieter. *"When I help my daughter Sierra learn the alphabet, I get anxious and demanding. It's over the top. It makes no sense, and it hurts her. She's trying so hard."*

I invited Ashley to close her eyes and recall a recent experience of helping Sierra. After a few seconds, her shoulders tensed and her jaw clenched.

"What are you noticing in your body?" I asked.

"I feel tight. Clamped up. Like I want to jump out of my skin. It's the same feeling I get when I'm with Sierra, trying to help her."

Then her eyes widened. *"Why am I like this? Am I just a demanding mom? What's wrong with me?"*

Ashley was in distress—and doing what many of us do when emotions overwhelm us: escape into thinking, explaining, and problem-solving. She was "in her head," trying to figure it out.

But the answer wasn't in her thoughts. It was in her feelings—and her emotional memory.

I gently encouraged her to return to the feeling. *"If you can, stay with it a little longer. Just observe what comes up."*

Several seconds later, her body jolted. Her eyes opened.

"Oh my God. That can't be it."

A childhood memory surfaced. When Ashley was learning the alphabet, her mom would help her. But her father often grew angry and scolded her mother: *"Why are you helping her? That's the school's job."*

An intense argument ensued. So decades later, when Ashley tried to help her daughter, her emotional brain remembered what her thinking brain had long forgotten.

"This is like the emotional learning we've discussed, but it's not about my performance anxiety. Whenever I help my daughter learn the ABCs, my brain recalls the experience from my childhood. But I don't know it. I mean, I didn't know until now. Just knowing that brings me a great sense of relief. So, I am not the terrible mother I feel I am."

Helping Sierra stirred up the same emotional associations that her brain had encoded long ago. Until she accessed that memory and learning and brought it into awareness, there was no way to shift her reaction.

Derrick Shuts Down and Withdraws

"Do you have a handout I can give my wife?"

That was Derrick's request during our tenth session. *"She sees the changes in me,"* he said, *"and she likes them—but she doesn't trust they'll last. Honestly, I don't blame her. I've tried before. It never stuck. But this somehow feels different. I feel like I've turned a corner."*

Derrick smiled, then paused. I flashed back to our very first session.

He'd come in anxious and discouraged, desperate to save his 14-year marriage.

"Whenever Marie talks about problems—whether it's with work, the kids, or between us—I just shut down. I pretend to listen, but she knows I'm not really there. Then I get up and walk away. She gets hurt. I get frustrated. I hate it. I don't want to shut down, but it feels like I have to. I've tried therapy before, but nothing sticks. Can you help me?"

Now, after nine sessions, Derrick was noticing something he hadn't felt before.

"I still need to practice the listening skills you gave me. But the difference is that now I can actually stay present. I don't feel that chest-pounding anxiety anymore. I'm just, I don't know how to say it, there. It's hard to explain. It's like a switch got turned off. Whatever we did—it worked."

His change was real. It wasn't just behavioral—it was emotional.

Like so many others, Derrick had spent years trying to change his behavior—the visible part of the problem—without ever accessing the emotional learning that caused it. He thought the issue was Marie's tone. Or the tension in their conversations. Or his lack of willpower.

As we worked together, Derrick uncovered the emotional learning behind his reaction. It came from his childhood, during long conversations with his mother.

"I had to sit still, be quiet, and pretend to listen to her complain about my dad. I did that so she wouldn't leave me like she left him."

That early emotional learning—the need to appear attentive to avoid abandonment—was still active decades later. Every time Marie brought up a problem, his brain detected a threat and deployed the same protective pattern: shut down, disconnect, withdraw.

When he updated that emotional learning, the anxiety faded. The need to withdraw dissolved.

The "switch" he felt turn off wasn't a fluke—it was a neural update.

(Note: Marie later worked on her frustrated reactivity, using the same five-step process that Derrick used and was able to update the emotional learning that had been fueling her frustration.)

Derrick's story—and those of many others—reminds me of the myth of Sisyphus: condemned by the gods to push a boulder up a hill, only to watch it roll back down, again and again.

That's what trying to change behavior without addressing emotional learning can feel like.

Learning by Association

Most of us think of learning as something deliberate—something we *choose* to do.

It is intentional and involves at least three key elements:

1. Motivation – a desire or need to acquire new knowledge.
2. Focus – conscious attention directed at the thing we want to learn.
3. Willpower – sustained effort to stay engaged through challenge or repetition.

When we activate all three, we say we're "applying effort." And neuroscience confirms this:

Energy follows focus.

But learning doesn't only happen when we intend it. The word association comes from the Latin *associare,* meaning "to join with." The brain learns simply by associating one thing with another—whether we intended to make that association or not.

This applies to both intentional and unintentional learning.

Intentional Associations

When learning is intentional, we direct our attention with purpose. Let's say you're planning a trip to Paris and want to learn French. You don't study Spanish—you choose French. You may use flashcards, language apps, or audio lessons to form associations between French words and their meanings. This is intentional associative learning.

Maybe you already know how to play golf and want to improve your putting. You don't start from scratch—you adjust your grip, stance, or routine. You consciously focus on the association between *how* you move and the result you get. That's also intentional learning.

We could even reduce this learning process to a simple equation:

- I want X → so learning Y will help me achieve X.

Unintentional Associations

Now contrast that with how most of us learn to avoid traffic at certain times of day, or how we instinctively pull our hand away from a hot stove, or how just the smell of morning coffee wakes us up. We didn't *choose* to learn these responses—they developed over time through repeated experiences. They are examples of unintentional associative learning.

Emotional learning is a powerful form of this. For example, have you ever met someone who said, *"I can't wait to get to work so I can feel anxious and incompetent!"* Or have you ever thought to yourself, *"I can't wait to go to the party so I can feel ignored and out of place"?* or *"It feels so good when I beat up on myself and reinforce my lack of self-esteem?"* Probably not. Most of us don't choose to do something because we want our emotional brains to learn something that involves pain and suffering.

Sometimes, learning to do something like running a marathon can be painful. However, you know it comes with achieving your goal. Pain and suffering are not what you are seeking.

Through experience and the emotions associated with experiences, the emotional brain forms patterns of associations like:

- Work and feeling inadequate.
- Conflict and feeling unsafe.
- Praise and feeling judged and rejected.
- Saying no and feeling loss and abandonment.
- Being seen and feeling humiliated and rejected.

These emotional associations are seldom rational—but they're deeply felt. And once formed, they often steer our lives from behind the scenes.

Emotional Learning Begins Early and Runs Deep

Most emotional associations are formed early in life—usually in the first fifteen years—when our survival depends on our connection to caregivers and our emotional world is still raw, unfiltered, and deeply impressionable.

In these early years, we don't have the cognitive skills to question what's happening or the context to evaluate whether something is safe. We simply absorb the emotional tone of our environment. We *feel*, and the brain records those feelings with what is happening to us and around us.

So when something painful happens—even subtly or repeatedly—your emotional brain may link that situation, person, event, or behavior with distress. You may not remember the event clearly. You may not even think of it as "trauma." But the feeling and what was happening when you experienced that feeling are stored as patterns of learned associations. This learning is implicit—outside of awareness, but still active.

The Emotional Learning of Shame and Writing, Revisited

As I shared earlier, my emotional brain had formed a strong association between writing and shame. That association wasn't only about the publishing process. It tapped into something deeper and older: emotional memories of feeling shame and the not-good-enoughness of a child growing up in an alcoholic family.

Without realizing it, my brain had created an association that it used as a prediction.

Writing = shame and rejection.

So every time I sat down to write, I wasn't just facing a blank page.

I was facing the felt memory of shame and rejection. To protect me from that pain, my brain responded the only way it knew how: with anxiety, resistance, and procrastination.

The same thing was happening to Ashley with the alphabet and to Derrick with his wife. A lack of insight, intelligence, or effort didn't cause their adult challenges. Emotional learnings acquired decades earlier drove them—learned truths that had become embedded in their nervous systems.

Until those learnings were brought to awareness and updated, they couldn't be changed.

Emotional Learning: An Unintentional Associative Process

By now, it's probably clear to you:

- **Emotional learning doesn't happen with intent or awareness.**
- **We don't *choose* what our emotional brain learns.**
- **We can only discover what it *has learned* through how we react.**

Throughout our lives, the brain quietly collects emotional information. It stores patterns that associate people, situations, or experiences with either **emotional reward** or **emotional pain**. And because this kind of learning is automatic and implicit, we don't realize it's happening.

We also don't realize what has been learned—until it's triggered. You might feel anxious, irritable, numb, angry, or ashamed as your protective behaviors kick in. These aren't overreactions. They're protective reflexes based on what your brain believes will keep you safe:

- *Even if the threat of pain is outdated.*
- *Even if the threat of pain isn't real anymore.*
- *Even if it was never real to begin with.*

Why Emotional Learning Feels So Real—Even When It Isn't

As we've seen in Ashley's and Derrick's stories, emotional learning doesn't just shape what we do—it shapes *how things feel.* That's what makes it so powerful.

When a pain-infused emotional learning is triggered, the associated threat feels present—even when the original experience is long past. You might *know* it doesn't make sense, but your body still reacts as if the danger is real.

That's because emotional learnings are stored in the brain's implicit systems—the same systems responsible for survival. These systems aren't wired to reason. They're wired to protect.

Your brain doesn't ask, *"Is this threat still relevant?"*
It asks, *"Have I seen this pattern before—and was it painful?"*
If the answer is yes, it sends a signal: *Protect yourself.*

It's not conscious. It's not rational. But it feels like the truth.

This is why people often say things like:

- *"I know I'm overreacting, but I can't stop."*
- *"I know this isn't about my partner—but it still feels like it is and gets to me."*
- *"It makes no sense that I feel this way."*

These are clues that you're dealing with an old emotional learning, not a current reality.

Summary

This chapter explored the nature of *learning from experience*, emphasizing the powerful role of emotional learning. It distinguished between intentional learning, which is conscious and effortful, and unintentional learning, which happens unconsciously through emotional associations that are encoded as emotional learnings. It discussed how these emotional learnings shape behaviors and reactions.

Looking Ahead: From Learning to Unlearning

We often think of learning as something we do on purpose. But emotional learning is different. **It happens within us—quietly, early, and deeply**. Once learned, these emotional associations shape our reactions, limit our behavior, and generate protective patterns we mistake for personality or fixed traits.

But here's the good news:

- What's been learned can be unlearned and updated.

- Your brain's protective system can be optimized to enable you to do the unlearning and updating process.

In the next chapter, we'll explore how this process works. Specifically, we'll look at:

- Why emotional learnings feel true, even when they aren't.
- How your brain's **survival bias** can make past pain feel present.
- And how to begin identifying the emotional patterns behind the problems you want to change.

We're not just learning about triggers—we're learning how to free ourselves from them.

Chapter Three
Emotional Learning:

How We Acquire Knowledge
About the Third Dimension of Our
Human Experience

"The more intensively the family has stamped its character upon the child, the more the child will tend to feel and see its earlier miniature world again in the bigger world of adult life. Naturally, this is not a conscious, intellectual process."

This observation, attributed to esteemed 20th-century psychoanalyst Carl Jung, also describes the emotional learning process. But it is not just the family that does the stamping. Teachers, friends, classmates, the media, social media, online chat rooms, advertising, and various cultural influences also contribute to this process.

Chapters One and Two introduced you to this category of learning. I discussed how the emotional brain acquires knowledge about what causes pain and feels unpleasant, as well as what causes pleasure and feels pleasant. This chapter delves more deeply into the emotional learning process. This is important for two reasons:

1. Emotional learning is a process most of us are not familiar with, despite its powerful influence in our lives.

2. The contents, examples, and exercises I use in subsequent chapters build on having a basic understanding of how emotional learning (a process) creates an emotional learning (the outcome of that process) that becomes our triggers.

This chapter explores:

- The **Three Rs of Emotional Learning**
- The **Language of Feelings and Emotions**
- **How Emotional Learning Happens.**

You will also meet Suzanne. I wrote about her in my first book, *Reclaiming Your Self.* It is about an interaction she had with her father on the beaches of Kauai. When I wrote that book, I knew little about implicit emotional memories and nothing about emotional learning. For illustration purposes, we will follow Suzanne's journey to become trigger-free in subsequent chapters.

The Three Rs of Emotional Learning

You may have heard the 1907 song *"School Days"* by Will D. Cobbs and Gus Edwards, celebrating the traditional three Rs—'Reading and 'riting and 'rithmetic. Similarly, the emotional three Rs—Rules, Roles, and Relating—are crucial, though less consciously learned. Embedded in our family and cultural systems, these Rs minimize emotional distress for caregivers and authority figures. They also perpetuate generational patterns.

For instance, I learned early to hide the shame of having an alcoholic father. I adopted roles—such as Mr. Nice Guy and family hero—to mask this shame. Family rules, like ignoring my father's drinking or never discussing it, reinforced this emotional learning.

As you read the following descriptions of the three Rs, I suggest making notes about any information that intellectually or emotionally resonates with you. This information may be helpful when you apply the five-step transformation process in Chapters Eight through Eleven.

Rules

Explicit societal rules, like traffic laws, protect individuals. In contrast, implicit emotional family rules safeguard caregivers from distress rooted in their past. These covert rules, communicated subtly through behavior or comments, significantly shape children's perceptions.

Imagine this scenario: Izabel, a 9-year-old girl, comes home after school and tells her mother, Josie, that she has been invited to a weekend overnight with other girls. As she talks about the girls who are going, Josie starts to feel an anxious uneasiness in her stomach, combined with feelings of shame and inadequacy because she feels that the other girls are from wealthier families. To relieve her distress, she tells Izabel, *"No, you can't go. They aren't very friendly people, and I don't want you to feel like you don't belong."* Josie may or may not be aware of an implicit family rule, "Don't do anything that could cause others to judge us in a bad light," an emotional learning from her own childhood experiences. As Josie acts to protect herself from the distress of violating an old family rule and the shame that the rule was intended to avoid, Izabel may also be learning something about whether she can trust herself and her feelings—the other girls are friendly and Izabel enjoys being with them—but her mother tells her they are not pleasant people.

Family rules tend to cluster around behavior associated with protective patterns, such as denial, pretending, silence, minimization, and control. Some common ones I've heard would read like the following list if they were written out. However, they are seldom written out, and others' actions enforce and reinforce them.

"You must never embarrass the family; otherwise, we will all be laughed at, shamed, and rejected."

"You must make us proud by always being the best, or you will disappoint and hurt us."

"You must follow the Church's principles, or you won't be worthy of God's love."

"You must not do anything that upsets your mother because if you do, it will be your fault, and you will be in a lot of trouble."

"Listen to and do what I say, or you will be sent to your room for a long time."

"Don't ever talk about yourself because it means you are selfish."

"You must hide your bad feelings because we all want harmony, and if there isn't harmony, it will be your fault."

"We don't talk about problems, period!"

"We take care of our own. You can't rely on anybody else because they will hurt you."

"People who don't believe what we believe are dangerous and are not to be trusted."

"Being together is the most important thing, so you better not do or say anything that threatens that."

Yes, all human systems need mutually agreed-upon and clearly stated rules; otherwise, society would descend into chaos. The critical difference between societal and emotional rules is that societal rules are created to protect individuals from harm and create stable, predictable human systems. They are also codified. **Emotional rules are designed to protect the rule makers from emotional pain that is anchored in their past.**

The exercise in the text box asks you to reflect on the subtle rules that may have been embedded in your family's emotional process.

> What implicit family-of-origin-based emotional rules do you feel or think you follow today that inhibit you from experiencing the life, love, and success that you desire? How do you know when to follow these rules? I suggest writing them down to bring them clearly into your awareness. This information may become helpful when you come to Part II and implement the five-step transformation process.

Roles

Roles have a primary function in emotional systems, such as families. They enable children to adapt to their emotional world as they experience it. The "assignment" of roles is not a conscious process or the outcome of a family meeting. Instead, family members learn to take on specific behavioral characteristics to adapt to their family's emotional process.

- Hero: I maintain my self-worth through achievement and looking like I have my act together to avoid feeling shame and not being enough.
- Caretaker: I focus on keeping things going and looking normal to avoid feeling the pain of disapproval and rejection.
- Scapegoat: I take the blame for problems to keep the focus off problems, so I don't feel rejected or abandoned.
- Rescuer: I focus on helping others to avoid the discomfort of powerlessness.
- People Pleaser: I focus on pleasing others and being nice to avoid the discomfort of conflict or tension.
- Clown: I provide comic relief during stress, conflict, and tension to distract myself and others from discomfort.
- Tough Guy or Gal: I maintain an image of strength to avoid helpless feelings and anxiety.
- Rebel: I go against rules, authority, and structure to cope with feeling powerless.
- Perfectionist: I focus on being perfect in everything I do to control the shame and anxiety of being seen as imperfect.
- Victim: I focus on a sense of powerlessness to avoid feeling the pain of being alone and helpless.
- Martyr: I derive a sense of self from giving up my needs, so I don't feel ignored or rejected.
- Saint: I focus on being good, righteous, and meek to avoid feeling shame and unworthiness.

A few questions to consider: Do you identify with any of these roles? How does that role show up today? What family dynamic do you think contributed to you taking on that role? What do you feel would have happened in your family or to you if you stepped out of that role?

Relating

The third R concerns two patterns of communication and relating: shutting down communication and the mixed message.

Shutting Down Communication

Families often have rules for withdrawing from or avoiding uncomfortable emotions by shutting down open communication. This usually results in a "damned-if-you-do" and "damned-if-you-don't" feeling. For example, imagine the feelings of a seven-year-old who hears the following question after she says something that upsets her mother: *"What you said upset mommy. Don't you love mommy? Why would you say something to upset her?"*

Remember the adage, *"Children should be seen and not heard?"* The implication is obvious. The modern interpretation is *"Don't say anything that makes anyone uncomfortable."* It is hard not to do, especially if you never quite know what makes people uncomfortable until you learn.

Mixed Emotional Messages or 'Speaking with a Forked Tongue'

Speaking with a forked tongue is an old idiom that refers to deceitful and manipulative communication. It is the mixed emotional messages that are often inherent in families that have shame-based histories, such as addictions. They can take various forms, but they tend to follow a basic pattern: the message and the feelings associated with communicating the message are inconsistent. For example, the parent who combines a message of love with a touch of guilt, *"I am doing this for you, and I hope you are grateful because I love you so much,"* or the phrase, *"This hurts me more than it hurts you"* as a child is being punished with isolation or physical abuse.

There are many variations of this template: A misalignment of nonverbal communication (tone of voice, facial expressions, and body posture) with verbal communication (words spoken) that creates emotional and cognitive confusion in the person who receives the message. These ways of relating are similar to some protective behaviors we use to avoid emotional pain, such as denial, pretending, withdrawal, minimization, and rigid control.

This is a question for your consideration: What do you think the emotional brain learns about relationships, communication, and love when it experiences these kinds of emotionally confusing ways of relating and communicating?

Understanding Emotions and Feelings

I have used the terms 'trigger', 'emotional learning', and 'the feeling of what will happen' synonymously because they all refer to the same phenomenon: the implicit memory of an experience and its associated emotions.

In Chapter Two, I referred to emotion as the experience of being stirred up. A feeling is an emotion with an added dimension of awareness. One of the origins of the word feeling refers to understanding. When we understand an emotion, we can give it a name.

For example, several years ago, I was attending a workshop. In one of the training exercises, I experienced an emotional sensation that felt like Champagne bubbles in my chest. I had felt it before, but for the first time, I could put a name to it. It was the experience of delight! Since then, I have been able to understand what I was feeling when that emotion emerges within me.

I bring the difference between an emotion and a feeling to your attention because when we have an experience based on old emotional learnings, we often struggle to explain how it feels or put words to it. This inability to understand or put words to emotions and physical sensations is so common that we've collectively created idioms to communicate our experiences:

"It feels like the other shoe is going to drop."
"I feel stuck between a rock and a hard place."

"I'm damned if I do and damned if I don't."

"I have to walk on eggshells."

"I always come up short."

"I always get the short end of the stick."

"It's the calm before the storm."

"When it gets too good, something bad is just around the corner."

"I better not rock the boat or make waves."

"I feel like I'm on top of the world."

"There's light at the end of the tunnel."

"It's a piece of cake."

"Every cloud has a silver lining."

"It's time to bite the bullet."

> You may have used some of these idioms to describe your emotional states. Go back and review the list again and select your favorite or one you are familiar with. Can you recall a situation in which you used that idiom to describe your experience, and if you do, what are you feeling as you do?

How Emotional Learning Happens

So, how does this emotional learning process take place? Before we explore that question, I would like to provide you with a simple illustration of the triune brain structure with which we are familiar. Although the triune brain model is being refined, I will use it in the interests of simplicity

Illustration 3.1 – The Basic Triune Model of the Human Brain

Have you ever experienced the "head-versus-feeling" conflict? It occurs when the thinking brain possesses knowledge that does not align with the knowledge held in the emotional brain.

Thinking Brain
The thinking brain is the most recent addition to the structure of the mammalian brain.It is responsible for language, planning, higher-order thinking, perception, problem-solving, and the conscious learning process.

Emotional Brain
The emotional brain, also known as the limbic system, is believed by neuroscience to be responsible for emotions and motivations such as nurturing, reproduction, affection, socializing, and the unconscious emotional learning process.

Reptilian Brain
The reptilian brain is the most primitive part of the brain. It is responsible for our oldest and most primal drives, such as aggression, dominance, and protection.

I now want to introduce Suzanne. As I mentioned earlier, I will be using her story throughout the book to illustrate the emotional learning and triggering process, as well as the five-step transformation process.

Suzanne's Emotional Brain Learns Something about Asking for What She Wants

As you read this brief vignette, notice your emotional reactions. Please keep in mind that I am attempting to apply a linear, mechanical description to a non-linear, neurobiological, organic process that happens within the brain in milliseconds.

Sunny skies. Warm breezes. The sounds of adults and children playing in the Hawaiian surf. Snorkeling gear flopped on feet and dangled on rocks. Music. Picnics.

A family—a father, a mother, a young boy about eight, and a girl about six—is spending the day at the beach.

Suzanne, the little girl, is playing near the surf. She finds something in the sand and runs up to her family, excitedly holding a little shiny stone, her treasure.

"Look what I found!" she exclaims, her smile radiating with the glow of her achievement. *"I want to take it home!"*

"No, put it back!" her father says, his words shooting like darts aimed at a target.

She flaps her arms wildly for a few minutes as a grimace of pain washes over her face.

"Please. I found it!" She holds it up to show her father.

"I said, 'No!' Now put it back." The words bite into her. *"Get ready to go. I'll either take you or the stupid stone."*

Suzanne feels the delight of her desire to take her treasure home. She also feels the biting reaction of her father. She turns away from him, her shoulders slumped, resigned to her task, and puts the stone back gently where she found it, saying goodbye to this treasure she will never see again.

Illustration 3.2 illustrates how Suzanne's emotional brain acquires knowledge about asking for what she wants.

What did you notice happening in your body as you read this? What do you think Suzanne's emotional brain may have just learned about asking for something she wants?

Illustration 3.2 - The Basic Implicit Emotional Memory and Learning Firing and Wiring Process - Suzanne's Experience

The numbers in the illustration correspond with the explanations below.

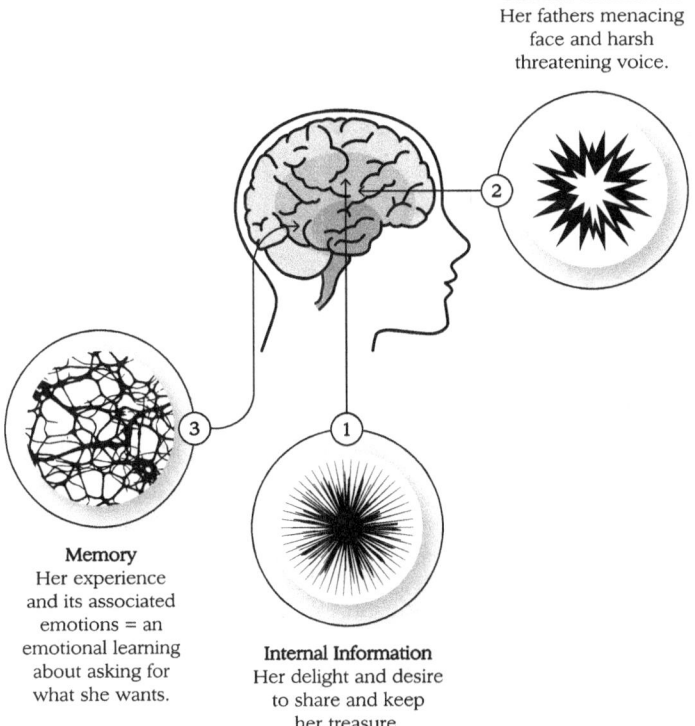

External Information
Her fathers menacing face and harsh threatening voice.

Memory
Her experience and its associated emotions = an emotional learning about asking for what she wants.

Internal Information
Her delight and desire to share and keep her treasure.

1. Suzanne is stirred up by emotions of delight and excitement at finding and wanting to share her treasure with her family. She shows it to her parents and asks if she can take it home.

2. Suzanne's father reacts with strong, angry emotions and aggressive verbal communication. His menacing face and the emotional force and tone of his voice stimulate her body's fight-or-flight response. She is flooded with a wave of terrifying feelings as adrenaline and cortisol rush to her body's rescue.

3. Neurons fire and wire in her brain as this emotionally intense, threatening interaction becomes an emotional memory. Her emotional brain acquires knowledge associated with the pain and suffering of asking for something she wants. That memory and its associated learning are 'stored' in the sub-cortical regions of Suzanne's emotional brain.

Suzanne's experience with her father becomes an implicit emotional learning—an encoded pattern of acquired knowledge about the pain and suffering associated with asking for what she wants. However, she is not aware that this learning is happening or what she is learning.

Let us imagine that this was a one-time event and that her father later apologized for his behavior, comforted her, and helped her find a new treasure. What would her emotional brain learn then? She might learn that people make mistakes, but that, in the end, it's okay to ask for what she wants.

However, what if this was her father's frequent behavior pattern when she asked for something? Her emotional brain would continue to learn that asking for something she wants and expressing herself is dangerous and painful, and associated with the terrifying threat of abandonment. To help her adapt to her world, avoid pain, and survive, she might become the child that parents often describe as no trouble, quiet, sweet, always helpful, and never making a fuss. The perfect child!

As I mentioned previously, we acquire most of our implicit emotional memories and learnings in the first fifteen years of life, when learning how to adapt to survive is crucial. This is not a conscious process, and bringing these learnings into conscious awareness so that they can be updated is not about blaming parents for their mistakes and shortcomings. Consider this: blame is a protective behavior, and they also have their own pain-infused implicit emotional learnings that, when activated, cause protective maladaptive behaviors.

This work is about becoming aware of what we have learned that gets in the way of the life we desire to experience as adults. The way to do that is to become aware of and update emotional learnings that no longer serve us.

Summary

This chapter explored how emotional learning profoundly shapes human experience. It discussed the implicit rules, roles, and relational patterns within family and cultural systems. This learning process occurs largely unconsciously and influences how individuals perceive and interact with the world, often perpetuating generational emotional patterns.

A Dilemma We All Share

This is the dilemma we all share. As Jung's quote at the beginning of this chapter suggested, **we unconsciously 'see' and 'experience' the miniature world of our childhood in the larger world of adulthood.** The process responsible for this *is **our unconscious remembering process.*** We will explore that topic in the next chapter.

Chapter Four
Recalling to Mind:

How the Brain Remembers
What We Don't Know We Learned

What comes to your mind when you think about the words memory and remember? Given the media's attention to memory impairment, your initial thoughts might involve strengthening your memory or recalling experiences with loved ones who are affected by memory issues. The word *"remember"* originates from the Old French *remembrer* and Latin *rememorari*, meaning '*to recall something to mind.*' In his book, *Searching for Memory*, I believe Daniel Schacter captures the broader meaning of these terms: *"Our memories are the fragile but powerful products of what we recall from the past, believe about the present, and imagine about the future."*

This book focuses on emotional memory and learning, triggers, and becoming trigger-free, and this chapter addresses:

- The difference between **explicit and implicit memory.**
- The **conscious and unconscious recalling-to-mind** process.
- The role memory plays in the **brain's survival bias.**

Acquired Knowledge Becomes Memory

Chapter Two described 'learning from experience' as 'acquiring knowledge as an outcome of what we go through.' It is a knowledge acquisition process that can be conscious or unconscious. The knowledge that we acquire, especially when it is associated with intense emotions, can become a memory. My experience as a psychotherapist suggests that most of us are more familiar with explicit memory than implicit memory. Therefore, I would like to briefly review the differences between them before discussing the significance of the implicit nature of emotional learning.

Explicit Memory

If I ask you to recall an exciting event from high school, you might remember several and then focus on one that resonates the most. You could describe some aspects of the event, like where it happened and who was there, and you might even feel some of the same emotions that were stirred up at that time. This is an example of an episodic memory. As you recall episodic memories, you may also feel some of the feelings that you experienced at that time. I referred to this phenomenon in Chapter One as state-dependent memory: when we remember events, the brain also recalls the emotional experience encoded within the memory network.

Another form of memory, called semantic memory, encompasses knowledge, facts, and information. For example, this book contains much information that you may have learned already and might recall as you read it. The act of reading itself depends upon your knowledge of the meaning of words and sentence structure.

Is semantic memory also state-dependent? Consider Ashley's anxious ABCs from Chapter Three. Ashley's semantic memory of learning ABCs became entwined with painful emotions due to her parents' conflicts. She could use counteractive measures to cope with and manage her reaction, but that would interfere with teaching the ABCs. Until she brought that implicit emotional learning into her conscious awareness and updated it, she was stuck with it.

Recall my experience with writing. My emotional brain had associated the semantic memory of writing a book with the intense emotional experience of shame and inadequacy. Voila! My emotional brain had learned that writing is painful and reacted to protect me from those toxic emotions. You may also feel discomfort and distress when you recall semantic learning experiences. For example, it is not unusual for some of us to react negatively to subjects such as mathematics, physics, and statistics because of our learned negative associations.

Implicit Memory

When you recall an episodic memory, you know that what you were experiencing in the present is the memory of a past event. It is explicit. Another category of memory, implicit memory, can be divided into two categories. One is called implicit procedural memory and learning, and the other is implicit emotional memory and learning. I will discuss implicit procedural memories first because they are the most familiar to us.

We use implicit procedural learning hundreds of times a day without any conscious recall. Consider a simple category one skill, like using a fork. As simple as the skill of using a fork seems to be for those of us who have been using one for years, there was a time when we didn't know how. Through repetition—recall the popular idiom, 'Practice Makes Perfect'—the how-to-use-a-fork knowledge became what memory researchers call implicit procedural memory. If we had not committed that learning to implicit memory, we would need someone to show us how—or read "The User's Guide to Using a Fork"—every time we wanted to use one. That would make for very long dinner parties. But we don't even have to think about it. We pick up the fork and enjoy our food. However, if I asked you to teach me how to do it, you could do that because the learning is not unconscious; it is subconscious.

Our daily life depends upon countless implicit procedural learnings stored in our brains, such as how to read, write, fry an egg, drive a car, and numerous other skills that we perform without conscious thought. Implicit procedural learning operates automatically because the brain has acquired the knowledge to perform specific actions without you needing to recall them consciously. Imagine a list of all of the things that we do that rely on implicit procedural learning; it would be very long.

As I mentioned in Chapter One, emotional learnings are linked to emotionally intense experiences, often, but not always, acquired unconsciously as an outcome of our early life experiences. Because we usually have no conscious memory of these experiences and their associated emotional learnings, we are unaware of how they influence our present-day lives.

The Conscious Recalling-to-Mind Process

When you consciously direct your brain to recall a memory, it functions like an Internet search engine. It is a process that I refer to as 'neuroogling'. (You won't find that term in the dictionary.) The brain searches for patterns of stored information that are similar to the incoming information, which enables it to make sense of what it perceives. When it finds a relatively close match, it activates that memory. You have then recalled to mind what you want to remember. Doing this enables you to navigate the world of people, places, time, and things. It is a crude pattern-matching process.

For example, as I type these words, my brain is neuroogling to find words in long-term memory to help my working memory assemble the sentences that I am typing on my keyboard. Am I aware that my brain is performing its neuroogling thing? No. However, I know that it is happening because I see the outcome on the page, where typed letters form words that become sentences, paragraphs, and chapters that will become the book you are now reading.

The brain uses cues, such as thoughts and images about what I want to communicate, as input to its neuroogling process. To me, the whole process is one of the beautiful mysteries of evolution.

A cue is anything that acts as a stimulus for something to happen. Actors use cues to enter their roles. High-performance athletes use mental and physical cues to set themselves up for what they are about to do. Alarms on your cell phone and calendar pop-ups on your computer all serve as reminders to alert you to an upcoming event or activity. Mnemonics—remembering things through words or memory cues—can often help us recall specific information. Then, of course, there is the infamous to-do list.

The following exercise is designed to demonstrate how the brain uses cues to launch the neuroogling search process. As you perform it, imagine yourself observing the process that is happening in your brain as it searches for the information you want to remember.

Recall a recent experience of being triggered. I suggest choosing one that is low on the emotional distress scale (like the pain scale your doctor uses), perhaps a rating of 3 to 4 on a scale where 1 is neutral or calm, and 10 is a strong negative emotional response. Before you do, note how you are directing your brain to recall that memory. What cues did you use to launch the recall process? Was it who was involved, or what someone said or did, or both?

Now, sit with that memory and pay attention to whatever thoughts, feelings, and images are coming up. Can you identify other cues embedded within the memory? Maybe you are becoming aware of something you thought or thought another person thought about you. For example, you may have recalled a scene in which your manager told you that you made a huge mistake that would take hours to rectify. You felt admonished and ashamed. Your cue to access that memory was recalling the scene in your office. However, as you sit with it and let the memory tell its story, you notice that it was your manager's tone of voice and intense stare that were the triggers that created your distress.

We will use this process as part of the five-step update process in Part II. Now, let us look at unconscious remembering.

The Unconscious Recalling-to-Mind Process

Unconscious remembering may seem like a contradiction in terms. After all, isn't remembering something that we do consciously? We have already discussed implicit or unconscious procedural memory and its significance. The same cue-based neuroogling process that enables us to access procedural memories takes place when the brain recalls implicit emotional memories and learnings.

Cues enter the brain as information, and the brain uses this information to search for and retrieve similar patterns. The primary difference between conscious and unconscious remembering is that you do not know that the brain has activated a memory because it is implicit. Think about the fork example I discussed earlier. We don't have to recall how to use a fork consciously; the cue of seeing it and picking it up to eat food is sufficient to activate the procedural memory of how to do it.

According to Daniel Schacter, a noted memory researcher, **we can be influenced by memories of past experiences without consciously recalling them**. It seems that the brain is very good at doing two jobs without our conscious participation:

1. Helping us navigate our daily lives (implicit procedural learning) efficiently and
2. Ensuring our survival by recalling what caused pain and suffering in the past (implicit emotional learning) to avoid it in the future.

The Brain's Survival Bias

Evolutionary psychology suggests humans possess a built-in survival bias. According to Louis Cozzolino, **our brains prioritize survival over happiness**, continually scanning for threats. This explains persistent triggering despite consciously knowing there's no present danger.

Recall that Ashley is the mom who felt highly anxious and frustrated when she was teaching her young daughter the alphabet. Ashley's brain had learned to associate pain and distress with learning the ABCs. Every time she helped her daughter, Sierra, with the alphabet, she was also triggering the implicit emotional learning associated with the threat of her parents' fighting. Yes, Ashley's brain learned how to recite the alphabet, but it also learned that learning the alphabet was an emotionally painful experience of threat and danger.

When she wrote what felt like the truth within that triggered feeling, it read like this: *I must make sure nothing bad happens when I help Sierra learn the ABCs because if something bad happens, it will be my fault. I will be punished just like I felt when I was a little girl, when my mother and father fought whenever my mother helped me learn my ABCs.*

This doesn't seem to make sense from an outside perspective: How could anything bad happen when Ashley is helping her daughter learn the alphabet? The rational, logical, thinking brain doesn't understand this statement. However, it makes perfect sense to the emotional brain, and the threat feels real in her body. She was unaware of the learning that her brain was recalling.

Recall how Derrick's shutdown and withdrawal behavior was caused by his brain recalling to mind something that he learned as a young boy: *I must be quiet, sit still, and pretend I am listening to you, Marie, just like I did when my mother told me about all her problems with Dad. I had to do that with my mother so that she would never leave me like she left my dad. So today, I do the same with you whenever you talk about problems. I get anxious and pretend I am listening, just like I did with my mother. And if you get upset with me, I get up and leave. I would rather do that than risk you leaving me.*

His young brain protected him from the threatening feelings of being abandoned by his mother. Whether she would leave him or not was not the issue—that was what his young brain had learned.

At this point in our evolution, we cannot escape the brain's inherent survival bias. What does this mean for all of us? New neuroscience and its practical applications show us that we can leverage and optimize this survival-biased learning, prediction, and adaptation process. Until we do, the brain will continue to do its job and inhibit our desire to create enduring transformation and thrive. That is what happened with Suzanne.

Suzanne in Her Thirties

Suzanne, the little girl who wanted to take her treasured stone home, is now in her early thirties. She is building a career and establishing relationships. All is going well for her except for a behavior pattern that has become a problem. She becomes very anxious before she asks her friends or employer for anything, and as a result, she avoids and withdraws from expressing herself. It even happens when her friends ask her what she wants to do. She shrugs and says, *"Whatever you want is okay with me."*

She wonders what is wrong with her, especially when her friends ask her why she doesn't tell them what she wants to do when they are planning an outing, and why she always goes along with everybody as if she has no preferences.

Suzanne wonders why she feels so uncomfortable expressing what she wants to do, even with her good friends whom she trusts. At times, she feels mildly depressed about a behavior pattern that she cannot seem to break. She senses her friends' frustration that she cannot express what she wants, and is also aware that her manager's reviews of her performance have always included a question about why she doesn't express any interest in advancing herself.

She did two years of psychotherapy in college and learned some techniques to cope with the anxiety that she was experiencing at that time. It also helped her understand her family's dynamics. She realized that her family was often chaotic and unpredictable, and that as a child, she would often withdraw to her room to escape the noise and unstable dynamics. The tools that she learned in therapy to cope with and manage her anxiety—deep breathing, tapping on her knees, redirecting her focus away from negative thoughts, and taking a small dose of Xanax—still come in handy, and she avoids visiting her family unless she has to.

Given its survival bias, the brain does a threat assessment of all incoming information, looking for a close match to prior experiences and emotional learnings.

Suzanne's brain recalls what it learned about communicating her desires and expressing herself, as well as the threat and distress associated with that behavior, as shown in Illustration 4.1. Various situations and interactions can serve as input to Suzanne's brain.

Illustration 4.1 – Suzanne's Brain in Recall and Threat Assessment Mode

The numbers in the illustration correspond with the explanations below.

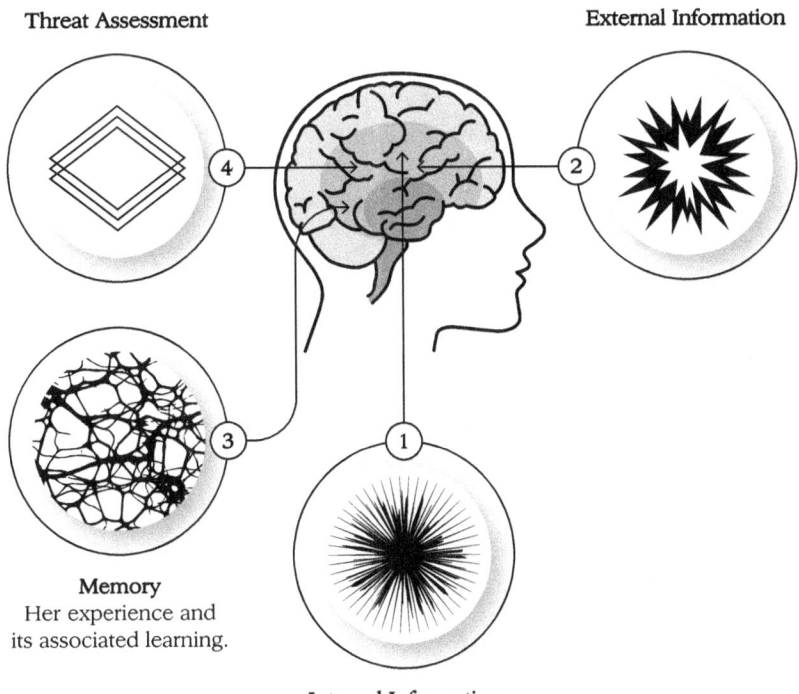

Threat Assessment

External Information

Memory
Her experience and
its associated learning.

Internal Information

1. Internal Stimulus - Suzanne feels motivated to express what she wants or her thoughts and feelings about something important to her.
2. External stimulus - Someone asks Suzanne for her opinion or preference. Examples might include her friends asking her which restaurant she wants to meet at for dinner, her boyfriend asking if she wants to go away for the weekend, or her manager requesting her input about a project.
3. The threat-infused emotional learning resides deep in Suzanne's emotional brain.
4. The Threat Assessment - The brain does its neuroogling search and screens incoming information for threats based upon what it learned in the past. Suzanne's brain recognizes a close match with what it has learned about stating her opinions or expressing her wants, as well as the threat of pain and suffering associated with that learning (3).

The outcome of that threat assessment is a prediction of imminent pain and suffering based on its past learnings.

Summary

This chapter discussed the crucial role that memory plays in our lives. It introduced the difference between explicit and implicit memory systems and the difference between conscious and unconscious recall of memories.

That brings us to another evolutionary marvel of the three and a half pounds of grey matter housed inside our skulls: *the predictive nature of memory.*

The Predictive Nature of Memory

Neurophysiologist Alain Berthoz states, *"The purpose of memory is not to let us recall the past, but to let us anticipate the future. **Memory is a tool of prediction**."* Our brain uses learnings from past experiences to predict future experiences. When these learnings are infused with pain, loss, fear, and danger, they become our triggers.

Upcoming chapters will explore how recognizing and updating these implicit emotional memories enables us to transform our emotional reactions and experience personal mastery and emotional well-being.

Chapter Five
If This ... Then This ... :
Your Predicting Brain Activates the Trigger

Unbeknownst to you, your brain's predictive nature influenced your decision to read this book. This prediction, however subtle, triggered a shift in your emotional state, prompting you to act. Just before this, something about this book piqued your interest. It could have been the title, the cover, or the brief description. Perhaps a friend gave it to you, and you decided to look at what it has to say. You may be seeking a change in your life, and your brain detected something about this book that you thought or felt could facilitate that change. That change may be as simple as satisfying your curiosity about what triggers are.

The language of predictions appears in many spheres of life. For example, sports commentators discuss predictions, and the sports betting industry is built around the prediction process. Pollsters take polls to predict the outcome of political races. Moreover, who doesn't listen to the weather predictions when planning an outdoor event? Our brain's predictive capacity enables us to adapt to our evolving world consciously.

This chapter examines:

- The crucial role that **our brain's predictive process plays in fulfilling its survival-biased functions**.
- The **conscious and unconscious prediction** process.
- The seemingly **irrational logic of the emotional brain**.
- The brain's **threat assessment** process.
- The importance of bringing the **threat predictions encoded within your triggers** into your conscious awareness.

If you are curious about the prediction your brain might have made about reading this book, take a moment to reflect on the following question:

What prediction might your brain have made about reading this book? Write down one thing you hope or expect to gain from it.

The Logic of a Prediction

During the formative years of our lives, we acquire the fundamental skills of reading, writing, and arithmetic. (While today's digital skills don't fit neatly into an 'R' acronym, they are just as essential.) Simultaneously, we absorb the three Rs of Roles, Rules, and Relating to adapt to our families and other social groups. This triple R "stamping process," as Jung called it, has been with us since Homo sapiens emerged as a species.

Back then, our unconscious emotional learning process centered on the question, "How do I fit in to meet my needs and survive?" That question is still with us today. My Mr. Nice Guy and Derrick's withdrawal behaviors may have worked to help us survive as children, but as adults, they are maladaptive. Ashley's anxious frustration with her daughter protected her from reexperiencing the terror that her brain learned to associate with learning the ABCs during childhood. At the same time, it caused great distress for her and her daughter.

Perhaps while reading this book so far, you have identified a protective behavior you want to eliminate. That behavior is the outcome of the brain's prediction process. We use that prediction process in both conscious and unconscious ways.

Conscious Learning and Predicting

Conscious learning is a process of acquiring knowledge focused on creating specific outcomes. In Chapter Two, I described the three elements of this intentional learning process. We feel motivated to learn something. Then, we focus our motivation on what we need to do to create our desired learning outcome and use willpower to maintain that focus until we achieve it. Until those outcomes become a reality, they are predictions of something we want to know or do in the future. Focusing on creating desired outcomes is probably the closest that we can come to shaping our futures.

Take a moment to think about any conscious learning endeavor that you have undertaken. Was it to advance your career, be a better parent, improve your golf game, deepen your spiritual connection, understand yourself better, overcome a challenge, cope with a health issue, or satisfy your curiosity about a specific topic? If you reflect on and examine any learning process in which you have engaged, you will realize that it involved predicting a future outcome. Think about it as a logic statement similar to the one that I presented above about acquiring this book.

If I learn ... (the knowledge that you want to learn), then I will be able to ... (the outcome that the learning will enable you to achieve), and that will help me to ... (the benefit you get by acquiring knowledge), (e.g., advance my career, be a better communicator, solve a specific problem, get recognition, have a closer relationship with ..., improve my health, hit the golf ball better.)

Some examples might include the following:

If I learn how to play Bridge, I can join a Bridge Club and expand my social network.

If I learn public speaking, then I can confidently present at work and advance my career.

If I learn meditation, then I can better manage stress and improve my overall well-being.

I doubt that you are consciously going through this prediction process when you feel motivated to learn something new or to reinforce or update something you've learned. However, you always perform one internal act regardless of the outcome or its focus: *you will conceive of a future outcome in your mind.*

Expectations and Plans are Conscious Predictions

When we plan an event or activity, we are using our brain's predictive capacities to focus our energy on creating a future outcome that we expect will come to pass if all goes as planned. Those plans are usually associated with positive expectations, and when they don't work as planned, we typically experience feelings that range from frustration to disappointment. We use this predictive capacity to plan everything from a simple trip to the supermarket to a complex retirement strategy.

Here are a few examples of what conscious predictions might look like if we wrote them out:

Desired outcome: *I want to celebrate my promotion by having a get-together with friends.*
Prediction: *If I ... (all the actions you will do to make that get-together happen), then everyone will have a great time, and I will enjoy myself and them as we celebrate.*
Action: *I take all of the necessary steps to make my celebration a success.*

Desired outcome: *I want to improve my golf handicap.*
Prediction: *If I use an 8-iron, I can probably make the green and putt for par, which should help improve my handicap. That will also help me improve my ability to choose which club works best under these circumstances.*
Action: *I use my 8-iron and see what happens.*

Desired outcome: *I want to go on a relaxing vacation in the sun.*
Prediction: *If I choose to vacation on Maui in October, it will be warm and give me the break I want.*
Action: *I plan the details and take my vacation.*

Once again, this is not a process that we usually write out in detail. We do what it takes to achieve the desired outcome. However, if I asked you to describe all of the steps you need to take, you could do it, even though it might feel strange and awkward, because going through that explanatory detail is not something we are familiar with doing.

Your brain's predictive function is also responsible for activating your triggers. If the brain recognizes the threat of pain and suffering based upon its threat assessment, it then predicts an imminent experience of the threat. When that happens, you are triggered! This is an unconscious prediction process.

The Unconscious Prediction Process

According to psychoanalyst and author Regina Paley (2008) and acclaimed neuroscientist Lisa Barrett (2018), *the brain is constantly making predictions using its past experiences as a guide to help us deal with the world around us and keep us alive.*

This prediction process enables us to adapt and survive! It is as if the brain is operating using a survival-biased prediction logic that might go something like this:

> *If ... (the action I want to do, or something happens that triggers me)*
> *then ... (the prediction of what your emotional learning tells you will happen to me.)*

Here are examples of predictions that clients identified when they brought the emotional learning—the trigger—into their conscious awareness. Unlike conscious predictions, unconscious predictions often emerge as subtle, hidden negative felt expectations that drive our behavior, as seen in these client examples:

> *If I assert myself, I will create conflict, and then people will reject me, and I will be alone in a dark world of emptiness.*

> *If I say no, then people will judge me as selfish and turn their backs on me*

If people compliment me and I accept it, they will think I am arrogant and full of myself and say bad things about me behind my back.

If I feel attracted to someone and get close to them, I will lose myself in feeling responsible for their well-being.

If people become interested in me and want to get to know me, they will see that I am a flawed, imperfect person who does not deserve any attention. They will reject me.

If people don't listen to me, it means I don't matter to them, and I will be all alone in an empty room.

When significant people tell me their problems and the problem involves me, I must find a solution because if I can't, I will be punished for causing pain to them and collapse into a heap of nothingness.

When I feel safe and things are going my way, then something bad will happen to me, and it is just around the corner. I will be hurt, and it will be my fault for not staying alert to the dangers around me.

These statements may appear irrational or immature, but they are still logical! They predict a painful future, albeit one that we naturally want to avoid. If you are wondering how something could be irrational and logical simultaneously, I will explain that in the next section. In the next chapter, I will pair the prediction statements above with their associated protective reactions.

The Seemingly Irrational Logic of the Emotional Brain

I worked in the computer field in my early twenties and recall the programmers discussing GIGO, a computer programming acronym that means 'Garbage In, Garbage Out.' It refers to how a computer program logically processes incoming data. It is an effective and viable program if the logic is tested and produces the intended output for a specific set of inputs. However, if the input you enter is faulty or incorrect, the output will be equally faulty or incorrect. Thus, regardless of how well the program runs or how sophisticated it is, if you put garbage in, you get garbage out. GIGO!

The emotional brain operates in basically the same way. It is logical in the sense that it applies what it has learned to determine the meaning of incoming information. Imagine someone becomes anxious around dogs after a single frightening childhood encounter. The prediction that 'all dogs are dangerous' is irrational but logically derived from personal experience.

Have you ever heard someone try to convince you that some self-critical thought you have about yourself is wrong? You know how ineffective the convincing is. You are in protective mode, and nothing they say will register as the truth as long as you are in this mode. You might even dig in your heels to prove that you are right about your feelings. After all, what you are saying about yourself feels like the truth! Here is a client story that illustrates this point.

I worked with a couple who were stuck in a pattern of arguing. They had been married for five years, and this pattern emerged during their second year of marriage. Mack was convinced his wife, Dee, was going to have an affair. Mack knew it was irrational, but it felt true. It was rooted in emotional logic. When Mack was young, his father repeatedly expressed strong distrust toward and disgust of women following his mother's affair. Although Mack consciously trusted Dee, his emotional brain insisted otherwise.

He identified a deep emotional learning that was the source of the prediction that women can't be trusted, and was able to share it with Dee: *Dee, I learned from my dad that women have affairs. Today, I feel that way with you, even though I know you would never have an affair. That is why I feel like I must never trust you.*

Although it was uncomfortable for Mack to write this statement down and acknowledge it as an emotional truth, it was what he needed to do to transform it and move on with his life and marriage.

There are three points that I want to emphasize about the information in this section:

1. When implicit emotional learnings are brought into your conscious awareness, they will often seem irrational while, paradoxically, being completely logical.

2. You will experience the irrational logic of the emotional brain (if you haven't already) when we get to the five updating steps in Part II. You will feel a conflict between your rational, logical thinking brain and your irrational, logical emotional brain. That feeling can signify that you are on to something in your quest to update an implicit emotional learning! It is lying just beneath the surface of your anxious feelings.

3. When you become aware of the pain-infused emotional learning, as Mack with his distrust of Dee, Ashley with her anxious ABCs, and Derrick with his need to withdraw from Marie, it will feel like the truth.

The Brain and Its Threat Assessment and Prediction Process

So, how does the brain know when to generate anxiety that signals an impending threat? Not only does the brain use its neuroogling process to make sense of incoming information, but I suggest that it also collapses time.

Our brain has a remarkable way of linking past threats directly to present circumstances, essentially 'collapsing' past experiences and future threats into a single moment of anxiety in the present.

Dr. Daniel Siegel (1999), a pioneering psychiatrist in the field of interpersonal neurobiology, infers that in his book, "*The Developing Mind.*" Experience creates memories, which in turn affect the brain. The brain then uses these memories to orient itself and navigate its interactions by predicting what will happen based on what it learned in the past under similar circumstances. *Moreover, the brain will alter its future responses as a result of how it is affected by its experiences in the present.*

Once again, we see that the brain either reinforces existing knowledge or revises and updates it with new information as a result of its experiences. This is how we learn from experience.

Let's look at this from a poet's perspective. Rainier Marie Rilke (1934) captured the essence of this process when he said, *"The future enters into us, to be transformed in us, long before it happens."* Almost a century after Rilke wrote these words, neuroscience has shown that the predicted future does enter into us via the brain's prediction process, even if ever so briefly.

I want to summarize their observations and the brain's threat assessment and prediction process in the following points:

- *When a pain-infused emotional learning (originating in the past) is activated in the present, the brain predicts an imminent future experience of pain and suffering based upon that learning—the brain recognizes the threat.*
- *The past experience and the prediction of future pain collapse into a felt experience of that threat in the immediate present.*
- *The brain's detection of that predicted threat in the present naturally generates anxiety.*
- *Anxiety activates protective measures to cope with the predicted threat.*

Suzanne's Brain in Prediction and Triggered Mode

Let's look at Suzanne's experience of the prediction process. Recall how Suzanne's experience as a young child with her father created an emotional learning that asking for what she wanted and expressing herself was a threat. Chapter Four described how this learning could be activated in real time by the brain's neuroogling and threat assessment process.

Illustration 5.1 illustrates how this process creates an imminent prediction of a threat that Suzanne feels in the present moment. Based upon that threat prediction, her brain turns on the threat signal of anxiety, and her body and brain must go into protective mode.

Illustration 5.1 - Suzanne's Brain in Threat Prediction and Triggered Mode

The numbers in the illustration correspond with the explanations below.

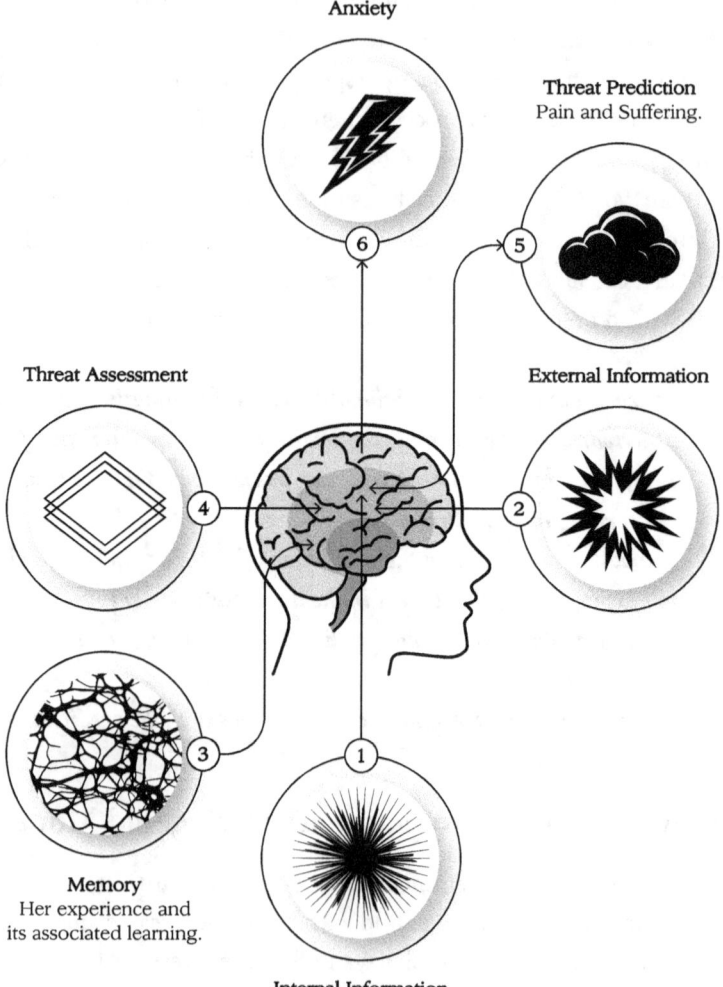

1. Internal Stimulus - Suzanne feels motivated to express what she wants or her thoughts and feelings about something important to her.

2. External stimulus - Someone asks Suzanne for her opinion or preference. Examples might include her friends asking her which restaurant she wants to meet at for dinner, her boyfriend asking if she wants to go away for the weekend, or her manager requesting her input about a project.

3. The threat-infused emotional learning resides deep in Suzanne's emotional brain.

4. The Threat Assessment - The brain does its neuroogling search and screens incoming information for threats based upon what it learned in the past. Suzanne's brain recognizes a close match with what it has learned about stating her opinions or expressing her wants, as well as the threat of pain and suffering associated with that learning (3).

5. The Threat Assessment predicts an imminent future experience of suffering based upon these past learnings.

6. Suzanne is triggered as the alarm signal of anxiety is activated. She experiences an ominous, anxious feeling with which she is familiar—it is the feeling of what will happen if she expresses herself.

Suzanne is not aware of what is causing her anxiety. However, she feels it, and in response, she may become stuck in the never-ending why of trying to understand where its source is. Alternatively, she might try a top-down approach to change, like taking a workshop on assertiveness, using affirmations, or focusing on positive thinking. She may even see a psychotherapist to explore what's going on and attempt to get to the bottom of her anxiety and its related withdrawal and avoidant behavior. She may get temporary relief using counteractive approaches. Still, the real cause of her problems will stay buried within her emotional brain unless she becomes consciously aware of the emotional learning and updates it.

If the Brain Predicts a Threat, It Must Protect from the Threat

Before we proceed to the next chapter, I would like to highlight an interesting and important point. The title of this section implies that **the brain *must* initiate a protective behavior if it detects a threat**. My clients often push back when we discuss the imperative nature of the brain's survival bias and the strength of the protection mode that anxiety causes.

The suggestion that they 'must' or 'have to' do something that they recognize is not in their best interest is a foreign concept, even when there is evidence in their lives that this is happening. As we explore the emotional imperative of the brain's protective mode and the brain's survival bias and prediction process, my clients see the puzzle pieces fall into place.

For example, Steven, a 44-year-old dentist who was stuck in depression and experiencing several stress-induced physical problems, identified this emotional learning and its associated protective behavior.:

Prediction: *If I have a conflict with a staff member, they will think I am a cruel and mean person who is only concerned with myself. They will say bad things about me and turn away from me. When that happens, I will fail and end up with nothing.*
Protection: *I must avoid any conflict with any team member because if I have a conflict with them, I will lose everything. Instead, I go home and complain to my wife.*

Steven initially resisted acknowledging his avoidance behavior as mandatory. Yet after observing himself for four weeks, he realized he wasn't choosing avoidance—it felt like he had no other option. With that insight, he understood why he often went home frustrated, unintentionally burdening his wife with his distress.

Summary

In the chapter, you learned that our brains constantly predict future outcomes based on past experiences, enabling us to adapt and survive. This predictive function involves both conscious learning and unconscious emotional learning, including the activation of triggers linked to past painful experiences. Understanding these processes can help us recognize and update emotional learnings that cause anxiety and protective behaviors.

Prediction and Protection

In Chapter One, I provided a list of problems and symptoms that people often experience. While no one would deny these are problems, it is a significant shift in thinking to see them as solutions to another problem. However, that is one of the primary messages of this book.

In the next chapter, I will delve further into this topic. I hope that you are gaining a sense of what is happening with us humans, including our counterproductive and maladaptive behavior, and the profound influence that implicit emotional learning has on our physical, emotional, and mental well-being, as well as our capacity to thrive.

Chapter Six
Our Shared Dilemma:

When a Problem Is a Solution

Frequently, the very problems we want to eliminate are the same ones the brain uses to keep us emotionally safe.

At the same time, they can destroy lives and relationships, ruin careers, cause family strife, and create havoc in people's lives. They are very stressful and predispose us to a plethora of health-related issues.

So, what are they keeping us safe from re-experiencing?

I want to reiterate what I stated in the Introduction: The dominant paradigm that informs most psychotherapeutic, coaching, and self-help approaches is a counteractive approach, one that targets reducing and eliminating problems and symptoms, and establishing goals for behavior change. That is the conundrum that most of my clients experience when they learn about emotional learning.

Many have invested years in self-improvement work and therapy, yet report that, although they have experienced some shifts, nothing has permanently changed. After a few sessions, they come to understand **how their problems are their brain's way of protecting them from past pain and suffering that it was predicting would happen again in the present.** That is the focus of this chapter.

Recall my struggle as Mr. Nice Guy from Chapter One, where my inability to assert myself seemed like my core problem, and I resolved to fix it by becoming assertive. Obviously, that solution changed nothing. Further, even if I had said something and Jason had apologized, that would not have changed anything within me. The trigger, of which I was unaware—the emotional learning that predicted pain and suffering if I spoke up for myself—would still reside in my emotional brain. My protective behavior would be triggered again because, for my brain, it was serving an essential protective function.

The chapter will explore our shared dilemma by examining the following:

- The **threats our protective mechanisms shield us from experiencing**.
- The **three clusters of protective patterns**.
- Examples of the **prediction-protection process**.

Protection from What?

I have worked with scores of clients using the 5-step process described in this book. That experience has given me insights into the threats embedded within our emotional learnings. Below are five of the most significant threats we commonly encounter in childhood. They are often at the root of our protective behaviors:

Abandonment

Abandonment involves experiences of neglect or being left by loved ones for whatever reason. It is the profound loss of an essential connection. Emotional learnings associated with abandonment often include feelings of aloneness, insecurity, worthlessness, and mistrust of others. Abandonment strikes at the heart of our deep longing to belong.

Rejection

Rejection involves experiences of being dismissed, left out, ostracized, disregarded, or shunned. Rejection is one of the most common threats that my clients identify. Emotional learnings associated with rejection often involve sadness, unworthiness, shame, and inadequacy.

Physical endangerment

Physical endangerment involves experiences in which a person's physical safety is threatened. This includes witnessing physical violence, being physically or sexually abused, or being threatened with such abuse. Emotional learnings associated with physical endangerment often involve feelings of helplessness and anxious vigilance and can result in emotional states of depression and generalized anxiety. At its extremes, physical endangerment can lead to PTSD.

Engulfment

Engulfment involves experiences of being emotionally smothered or swallowed up by significant others. This may also include someone constantly invading one's space or disrespecting one's autonomy. For example, if a father becomes dependent on his daughter for emotional support, the daughter may feel engulfed by his behavior. Engulfment often results in feelings of distress with closeness and intimacy, difficulty establishing and maintaining boundaries, and acute anxiety about losing one's independence.

Betrayal

Betrayal involves experiences in which a person's trust in another person is violated. For example, children can experience betrayal when parents and other caregivers make promises and do not keep them, deny the reality of a child's memories and experiences, or, in extreme cases, abuse them physically or sexually. The aftermath of betrayal is often characterized by hypervigilance, feelings of rejection, and wariness of trusting again.

Given the pain and suffering to which these experiences refer, it is no wonder that the brain does all it can to protect us when the threat of re-experiencing them again is triggered.

A Perspective to Consider

As adults looking at the list of five experiences presented above, we often minimize the pain they involve because we have had to do that for decades to survive. Thus, it can feel overwhelming to experience them as an adult and simultaneously recognize that, as a child, **you could not express what was happening in your body and the terror you may have felt**. As a child, you would not have the words to do so. You might scream or, like Suzanne, withdraw compliantly. But **there was no way for you to discuss what was happening with those around you.**

I say this to highlight this fact: an adult's perspective of these terrifying experiences will be different from a child's actual experience, encoded as an implicit pain-infused emotional memory and learning. This is why working with a trained therapist may be essential to maintain a safe container in which to discover and shed light on our early emotional learning experiences.

Three Clusters of Protective Patterns

In Chapter Two, I referred to the origin of the word emotion as 'being stirred up' and discussed the influence of emotional experiences on our behavior.

We naturally invite, move toward, and seek interactions, activities, people, and situations that we learned stir up pleasurable emotions.

This section focuses on the behaviors and symptoms we use to do the opposite—they push away, withdraw from, and avoid interactions, activities, people, and situations that we learned stir up painful emotions. I will further break these clusters down into externally focused and internally focused actions.

Pushing-Away Patterns

External Directed

When our brains predict a painful emotional experience, we may resort to behaviors such as **criticism, sarcasm, blame, fault-finding, threats of emotional or physical harm, one-upmanship, and physical aggression to push away the perceived source of that distress**. Pushing-away patterns typically involve externally directed emotional pressure or, unfortunately, physical force.

For example, Karen is one of my dental coaching clients. She contacted me to work on her leadership skills, her frustration with employees, and her critical attitude towards them. She was also on a low dose of Prozac to help manage symptoms of depression. She discovered that any threat to her need for perfection triggered distress and drove her to push away the threat (i.e., an employee's lack of adherence to a protocol) by being harshly critical. Her need for perfection resulted from a rule she learned in her family: If you're not perfect, you're not one of us.

One of the most common patterns of pushing people away is overfunctioning—an anxiety-driven behavior in which we feel responsible for the thoughts, feelings, and behavior of others and thus seek to control their thoughts, feelings, and behavior. This behavior is an attempt *to push another person in the direction we think and feel will be best for them, even though we are doing it to push away what is causing us distress.*

Furthermore, we often justify push-away overfunctioning behavior as wanting to help and show care for others. However, those others seldom experience it that way—for them, it is controlling and often experienced as a loss of agency.

When individuals overfunction for prolonged periods, they are prone to developing depression or debilitating anxiety, especially when the focus of their overfunctioning is no longer within physical proximity.

Internally Directed

Pushing-away behaviors can also be internally directed. These behaviors help us to push away distressing negative emotions so we don't feel them. Examples include **intellectualizing feelings, spacing out, fantasizing, rationalizing, dissociation, and repressing (unconscious pushing away) or suppressing (conscious pushing away) feelings.**

For example, Danny was aware that he had to suppress his feelings around his family, particularly concerning his mother's drinking. It had been a family rule for as long as he could remember: Don't talk about mom's drinking. Now in his mid-twenties, he reports that he is very uncomfortable with anyone who drinks and often finds himself either avoiding parties where there is drinking or being there but needing to space out with marijuana or sometimes alcohol. He told me, *"If you can't change them, join them. I'd rather do that than be alone."*

Withdrawing-from Patterns

Externally Directed

In contrast to pushing-away patterns, which seek to push away the cause of anxiety or distress, withdrawing-from patterns are intended to reduce or eliminate the stimulus's adverse effect while maintaining contact. Externally directed withdrawing-from patterns include behaviors such as **humor, placating, denial, accommodating, pretending things are okay, anxious controlling, and addictions.**

For example, Jenny is a 39-year-old mother of two children. She also works part-time as an event coordinator for a catering company. Her primary concern was her unrelenting anxiety about trusting her husband to care for the kids. She acknowledged that he was a great dad and held up his share of maintaining the household. Still, she couldn't shake the feeling that she had to constantly oversee his actions and how he communicated with them. Her controlling behavior was taking a toll on her marriage as well as her emotional and mental health.

Internally directed

Internally directed withdrawal usually manifests as **self-deprecating, negative self-talk.** I refer to self-talk as emotional-thought patterns because it has both cognitive and emotional aspects—you feel the thought, and it feels true. Self-deprecating emotional-thought patterns can be quietly dominant in people's lives, and for this reason, I would like to discuss this topic further. I refer to them as **protective emotional-thought patterns.**

Protective Emotional-thought Patterns

Many of us have spent decades focusing on negative, self-deprecating emotional-thought patterns—they can be pretty painful and deeply ingrained in our brains. Thus, it can be a challenge to imagine how they can be a solution to a problem, especially when they feel true.

I invite you to consider this possibility. For example, if feeling that I belong meant telling myself I was unworthy, I'd unconsciously adopt that emotional-thought pattern to maintain the essential connection.

I have observed that our negative emotional-thought patterns appear to consolidate around the three primary interpersonal needs that Will Schutz (1994) identified and described in his Fundamental Interpersonal Relationship Orientation (FIRO) theory. These three interpersonal needs are **significance, competence, and acceptance.**

Significance

When we feel significant, we feel acknowledged, visible, respected, heard, or important. We feel significant when someone considers our opinions and thoughts, talks with us, and includes us in matters that affect us. When we feel ignored, excluded, unimportant, invisible, or like what we say doesn't matter, we feel insignificant. Some common emotional-thought patterns associated with insignificance are:

- No one ever listens to me.
- I don't count.
- I'll never be heard.
- I don't matter.
- People ignore me.
- What I say isn't important.
- I'm invisible.

Competence

Feeling competent is more than having the skills to do a job or perform a task. We feel competent when we feel we can cope with the world, use our abilities to satisfy our desires, and handle problems. We also feel competent when we can do our job well, feel adequate for the challenges of our work, and have a sense that we can influence the outcomes that affect us. We often describe a sense of competence as feeling adequate, able, secure, and confident. When we feel inadequate, incapable, and not enough, we feel incompetent. Some common emotional-thought patterns related to incompetence are:

- I'm a loser.
- I'm not competent.
- I'm not perfect.
- I'm not (good, pretty, attractive, intelligent, or something) enough.
- I'm not secure.
- I'm not safe.
- I'm not (something I'm supposed to be)

Acceptance

We feel acceptance when we feel loved, cared for, liked, appreciated, trusted, and accepted. When we feel accepted by others, we feel secure. When we feel unacceptance, we often experience feelings of shame, unlovability, unworthiness, and rejection. Some common emotional-thought patterns related to unacceptance are:

- I'm not lovable.
- I'm not likable.
- I'm not trustworthy.
- I'm not okay.
- People won't (don't) like me.
- I'm not (good, caring, lovable, smart, or something) enough.
- I'm not worthy of . . . (whatever the issue).
- I'm unworthy.

Protective Emotional States

I want to discuss two emotional states. The first is depression. I want to be clear that I am referring to what is often called an **exogenous depression**. An exogenous depression is caused by an external event or stressor that can usually be identified. For example, individuals who experience the loss of a loved one, their job, or a significant disruption to their life may develop symptoms of an exogenous depression. An exogenous depression is often accompanied by anxiety, persistent rumination, and reactivity.

This contrasts with an endogenous depression, referring to depressive symptoms that originate from within the individual. Various biological, genetic, and neurochemical factors can contribute to this type of depression. This assessment does not apply to anyone who is experiencing an endogenous depression.

I have observed that withdrawing-from behaviors can, over time, increase the chances of an individual developing exogenous depressive symptoms. I say this because I have worked with clients who thought that depression was their primary problem and then discovered that depression was an outcome of years of withdrawing-from behavior. Depression was not their protective reaction to being triggered; it was serving no protective function. It was only when they delved deeper into the depressive symptoms that they identified the real behavioral problem and the threat it was protecting them from experiencing.

The second protective emotional state I want to discuss is **anxiety**. Both hypervigilant and generalized anxiety involve excessive worry and a sense of dread or threat. Hypervigilant anxiety is typically associated with a specific threat and results in constant scanning and acute alertness for that threat. It is common among individuals who have Post-traumatic Stress Disorder.

Generalized anxiety involves persistent worry and an anxious anticipation of something bad happening. The focus of generalized anxiety is usually, as the term generalized implies, a broad range of life concerns and activities.

Avoidance Patterns

The last protective pattern I want to discuss involves avoidance behavior. This pattern is intended to create physical space between an individual and anything that triggers a painful reaction. For example, we may avoid social or family gatherings if we have distressing experiences in these settings. The rule of pretending all is well may be too stressful and stifling.

I have worked with and observed many individuals who have either cut off or been cut off by family members because of the discomfort of unacknowledged family issues. The cut-off is the ultimate form of avoidance and can create a pattern that spans generations.

When Prediction Meets Protection

In Chapter Five, I discussed the brain's survival-biased prediction process and provided some examples of how these predictions appear when we become aware of them. However, we are unaware of the brain's predictions until we bring them into the light of consciousness. Using the predictions from Chapter Five, the following are some ways that the protection patterns discussed in this chapter can manifest.

Prediction: *If I assert myself, there will be a conflict, people will reject me, and I will be all alone in a dark world of emptiness.*
Protection: *The way that I deal with the feeling of this threat is to withdraw into a shell of self-criticism and anger at myself. I will also quietly blame other people for not listening to me as a way not to feel the threat of being rejected. As a last resort, I will overfunction and do what I want them to do. I must never assert myself so I can avoid being rejected.*

Prediction: *If I say no, then people will judge me as selfish and turn their backs on me.*
Protection: *The way that I deal with the feeling of this threat is to go along with what people ask of me. If I can't do that, I feel so anxious that they will think I don't care; then I withdraw into a slump and drink enough so I don't have to feel so anxious about what they think. I must never say no, so I won't feel the pain of people turning their backs on me.*

Prediction: *If people compliment me and I accept it, they will think I am arrogant and full of myself, and say bad things about me behind my back.*
Protection: *The way that I deal with the feeling of this threat is by getting anxious, minimizing the compliment, and sometimes the person saying it. Sometimes, I laugh and tell them they don't know the real me. I will turn away as soon as possible to avoid looking at the person who complimented me. I must not accept a compliment even if I know the other person is sincere.*

Prediction: *If I feel attracted and get close to someone, then I will lose myself in feeling responsible for their well-being.*
Protection: *The way I deal with the feeling of this threat is to keep myself busy with friends and other activities. I know that when that feeling in my gut tells me to be careful, I must get distracted and involved*

in activities that exclude the person I am attracted to until they eventually leave the relationship. I must protect myself from getting too close to anyone to avoid losing myself.

Prediction: *If people become interested in me and want to get to know me, they will see that I am a flawed, imperfect person who does not deserve any attention. They will reject me.*

Protection: *The way I deal with the feeling of this threat is to keep a safe distance from people. I feel anxious when people are interested in me. I change the subject or tell them my life is everyday and not that interesting. If the anxiety becomes unbearable, I will leave where I am and walk away. I have been doing that since high school, and I'm lonely today like I was then. But I'd rather be lonely than risk being rejected because I am so flawed. I must make sure people never become too interested in me.*

Prediction: *If people don't listen to me, then it means I don't matter to them, and I will be alone.*

Protection: *The way I deal with the feeling of this threat is to get anxious and angry. I will sometimes go blank. It's like I'm not there. Sometimes, I get angry and tell them they're not listening. This is strong in my close relationships. I've told people close to me that I get triggered when they don't listen to me. It's like it's their fault if I get triggered. I must make sure people listen to me.*

Prediction: *When significant people tell me their problems, and I feel it involves me, I must find a solution because if I can't, I will collapse into a heap of nothingness.*

Protection: *The way I deal with the feeling of this threat is to get really anxious and worry about what I can do to fix their problem. I will become fixated on finding a solution, and if I can't, I will withdraw into a dark depression of self-hate. I must find a solution to people's problems.*

Prediction: *If I feel safe and things are going my way, then something bad will happen to me, and it is just around the corner.*

I will be hurt, and it will be my fault for not staying alert to the dangers around me.

<u>Protection:</u> *The way I deal with this feeling is to stay constantly alert and not trust anyone. I must always be alert for the dangerous people who lurk around me, especially when I feel good about my life.*

These examples are composites of what my clients have become aware of as they explored the meaning of their triggered reactions. Becoming consciously aware of the emotional learning within a trigger and the protective behavior related to that learning are essential ingredients in the update process. I think you would agree with me that the learnings I listed above need an update.

Suzanne's Brain in Protective Mode

Illustration 6.1 illustrates what happens when Suzanne's emotional learning is activated today and how her protective behaviors are triggered. In this illustration, Suzanne is still unaware of what that trigger is. I will introduce her protective behavior and the predicted threat it protects her from in Part II.

Imagine one of the following four scenarios. The first three involve external information, and the fourth is internally generated information:

- Suzanne meets with several of her co-workers, and they ask how she would like to participate in a work project.
- Her friends ask her where she wants to have dinner over the weekend.
- Her boyfriend wants to know if she wants to go to a concert or a comedy show.
- She wants to ask her friends for advice about moving into a new apartment.

Illustration 6.1 – Suzanne's Brain in Protection Mode

The numbers in the illustration correspond with the explanations below.

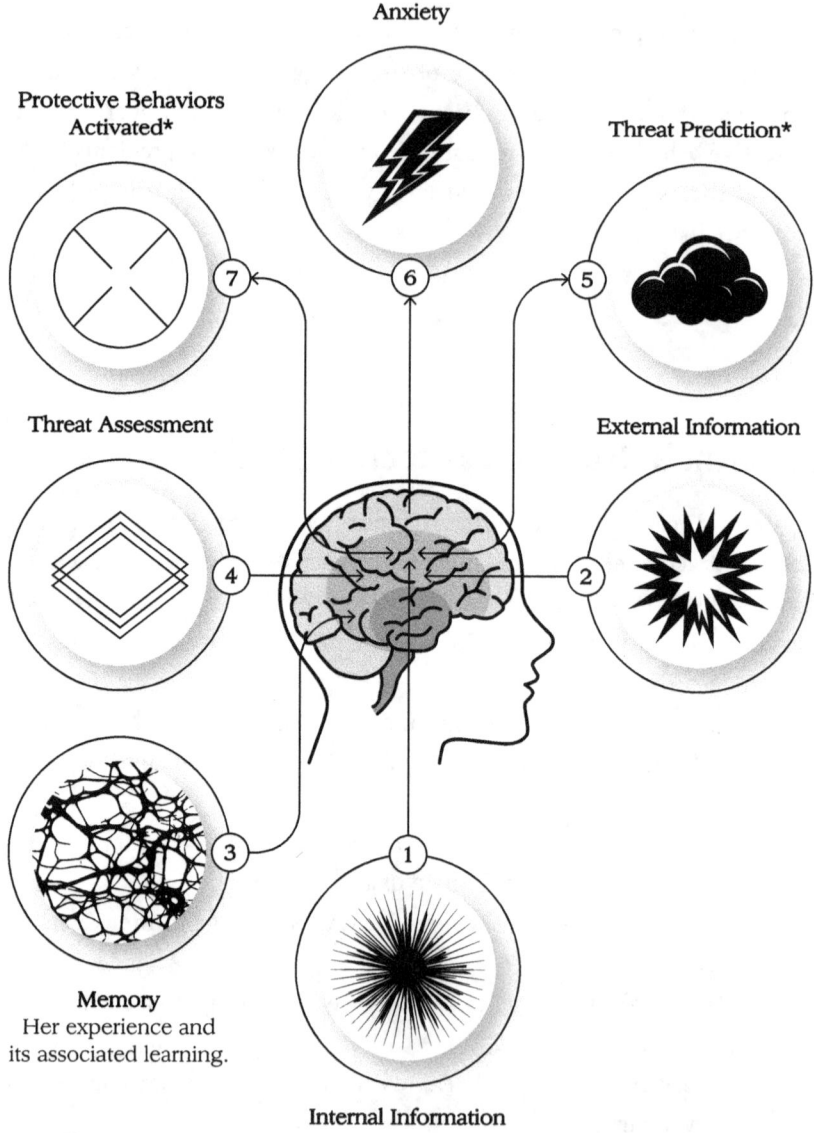

Anxiety

Protective Behaviors Activated*

Threat Prediction*

Threat Assessment

External Information

Memory
Her experience and its associated learning.

Internal Information

Suzanne's brain perceives (1) internal or (2) external information and does its (4) threat assessment using its past learnings (3) as input. The assessment process detects and triggers the emotional learning (3) that involves past suffering. Then, (5) it predicts an imminent future experience of pain based on that learning and turns on the alarm signal of anxiety (6) that activates her protective behaviors of withdrawal and accommodation (7).

The behavior that helped her avoid suffering as a child is now a problem for her. She experiences this behavior as something she must do. The sequence of experiences, from the brain's initial perception of the stimulus to the execution of the protective behavior, occurs within milliseconds and without any awareness on her part.

Creating the Difference that Makes the Difference

When we sincerely or desperately want something to be different in our lives, we are motivated to create that difference. Alternatively, we may resign ourselves to accepting what is. When it comes to changing behavior patterns, thought patterns, or emotional states, the dominant approach we use to effect change is to work on countering the identified problem.

However, this chapter demonstrates that the causes of most of our problems are implicit emotional learnings acquired without our awareness. My intention in Chapters One through Six was to explore this different way of thinking. It described and illustrated how our 20th-century counteractive approach will not create the difference that you desire.

Summary

The vast majority of our problems serve as protective mechanisms, shielding us from re-experiencing past pain and suffering. These protective behaviors, while intended to keep us safe, cause ongoing distress and dysfunction in relationships, careers, and health. The chapter explored the nature of these protections, the threats they guard against, and how they manifest in behavior and emotional states.

A Different Way of Thinking

In the next chapter, you'll learn a new way to think about protective behaviors—comparing them to the immune system—and learn about the five-step process that helps you uncover and eliminate the root cause of your emotional reactions.

Chapter Seven

Optimizing Our Brain's Learning, Predicting, and Adapting Process:

A 5-step Human Technology for Transformation

How do you think the world would be different today if our emotional evolution had kept pace with our intellectual evolution as measured by our technological advances?

In his 1990 book, *Flow—The Psychology of Optimal Experience*, Mihaly Csikszentmihalyi I think provides an answer to that question when he suggests that *our happiness and fulfillment depend not on mastering the world around us, but on how our mind interprets our experiences and how we master consciousness itself.* I suggest that we not only need to master consciousness, but also the unconscious realm of emotional learnings that are the filters through which our minds interpret our experiences. However, the neuroscience that enables us to master the unconscious was not known to us until the turn of this century.

Imagine this for a moment: You have identified a problem that is interfering with your desire and capacity to thrive. You could use individualized, programmed VR goggles to update the outdated, pain-infused emotional learnings causing the problem. We could accelerate our emotional evolution. Maybe then we would know, at both an emotional and cognitive level, the meaning of T. S. Eliot's famous quote: "*We shall not cease from exploration, and the end of our exploring will be to arrive where we started and know the place for the first time.*"

Until then, we can benefit from a human technology that optimizes our brain's survival-biased learning, prediction, and adaptation process. **We can choose to free ourselves from the emotional tyranny of past**

threats that no longer exist, yet still feel like they do. This chapter will introduce this technology by discussing the following:

- The **five steps to living a trigger-free life.**
- **Personal examples of applying the five-step process.**
- An interesting analogy that compares the immune system's protective function and what could be called **the brain's emotional immunity to change.**

Five Steps to Living a Trigger-free Life

The five steps of the human technology that optimizes the brain's survival-biased learning, predicting, and adapting process are:

Step #1 - *Clarify the Problem Pattern and Your Desired Change*

This step involves a two-part process: first, clarify the problem, and second, identify your desired change. I will discuss these in Chapter Eight.

Step #2 - *Discover and Clarify the Threat Prediction and the Protective Behavior You Use to Protect Yourself from the Predicted Threat*

This step involves discovering the threat prediction within the trigger that, when activated, causes the problematic protective behavior. The threat prediction is an explicit statement of the emotional learning that you acquired earlier in your life. This step is the essence of Chapter Nine.

Step #3 - *Observe and Validate What You Have Identified and Written*

In Step #3, you engage in observing the predicted threat and its associated protective behavior(s) in real-time or recall a triggering event or interaction to validate what you have written. Revise as needed to ensure its emotional validity. This step is also included in Chapter Nine.

Step #4 - *Identify and Clarify the Threat Prediction Correction Information*

The threat prediction you articulated and tested in Chapters Eight and Nine needs an update. This step involves identifying information and experiences that contradict and thus update the threat prediction. We will go over Step #4 in Chapter Ten.

Step #5 - *Make Your Brain Right by Making It Wrong—Pair the Threat Prediction with the Prediction Correction Information.*

This is the essential action step that makes enduring transformation possible. By pairing the threat prediction with contradictory experiences and information, you can cause the brain to update itself. Additionally, I recommend monitoring and observing the outcome as a felt experience, and continuing to update as needed, using the Trigger-informed Mindfulness process (Chapter Eleven). I will go into more depth about Step #5 in Chapter Eleven.

These five steps are based on the therapeutic memory reconsolidation protocol developed and taught by the Coherence Psychology Institute. I have adapted it for use in my work with clients and the intended audience of this book. To illustrate how these five steps work together, I will use my transformative experience at that November 2015 workshop.

Transforming My Toxic Procrastination

In Chapter Two, I introduced you to my ten-year pattern of toxic procrastination regarding writing. As I described in that chapter, I didn't know:

1. That my emotional brain had learned to associate writing with the pain of shame, rejection, and failure during the writing and publication of my second book, and
2. That procrastination was my brain's way to protect me from experiencing those feelings again.

Now, let me describe how, by engaging in these five steps, the threat was eliminated, and I was able to write again.

Many psychotherapy training workshops incorporate live demonstrations to illustrate new protocols, followed by practicums in which participants learn to apply these techniques in a hands-on setting. Thus, I knew I would have an opportunity to work on my procrastination problem when I attended the November 2015 workshop on the practical application of what was called Memory Reconsolidation. What I did not expect was to be the 'client' for the live demonstration of this human technology. Although I don't remember all of the details of the live sessions, three activities stand out.

Step One was clear to me. My problem was procrastination concerning writing, and, as I noted in Chapter Two, it was not just your 'setting things aside' kind of procrastination or what some might call 'writer's block'.

Step Two, discovering and clarifying the threat-infused emotional learning associated with writing, involved two actions. The first was to activate the anxiety and discomfort associated with writing. Keep in mind that I was unaware of the emotional learning that was causing that anxiety. I felt dread and anxiety at about six on an emotional pain scale of 1 to 10 (1 representing feeling calm and 10 being highly emotionally distressed). This recall process activated the emotional learning that existed in my emotional brain and was outside my awareness. By recalling the context in which the anxiety emerged, the trigger was activated, and my brain was predicting shame and rejection based upon what it had learned previously. (I can discuss that now as I look back at the experience and what I have learned about emotional learning and the predicting brain.)

There I was, sitting in front of dozens of peers, feeling and describing the visceral discomfort I had known for the past ten years. Memories of shame and feeling not good enough emerged as I recalled the rewrite process of my second book. Memories of childhood also flashed on the theater screen of my mind. I felt like I was drowning in a red river of shame. With the facilitator's guidance and encouragement, I was able to articulate a statement clarifying the meaning of the feelings that I felt beneath the anxiety:

> *I am certain that if I write what I want to write, I will be judged as a fraud and humiliated, and it will be my fault, just as I felt as a child who had to pretend everything was okay at home. I feel like I will drown in a red river of shame.*

The second action in Step Two was to describe the protective mechanism of procrastination:

> *The way I deal with this feeling is to become anxious and avoid writing by procrastinating. I find many excuses to justify my procrastination and beat myself up in the process. I would rather do that than feel the shame and rejection I am certain I will feel if I write another book and am seen as a fraud.*

With this written information, I could proceed to Step Three and test the emotional resonance of what I had written. I didn't have to be at home, sitting at my desk, preparing to write. As I imagined that scene, I felt the tightness and dread of anxiety. The threat prediction statement felt true to me! I had identified the emotional learning that I had been fighting to overcome for over ten years. **By engaging with and exploring my anxiety-driven procrastination rather than fighting against or overcoming it, I was able to identify the trigger.** With this information in hand, I could move on to Steps Four and Five and update what my brain had learned that I didn't know it had learned.

Step Four involved identifying experiences that contradicted the threat prediction statement. I recalled feelings of pride and accomplishment as I remembered instances where my peers and clients recognized and acknowledged my efforts. I remembered what it was like to persevere when I faced challenges. I felt a sense of pride in the two books that I had written, and I was aware of my deep desire to write more. This process culminated in developing a prediction correction statement that read like this:

However, I have many experiences in which I have been recognized and acknowledged for my workshops, writing, and presentations. I take responsibility for my actions and have never consciously and intentionally acted in any fraudulent way. I have always sought feedback to help me improve, and although it is sometimes uncomfortable, I have consistently benefited from it. I am also open to feedback and to learning from it. I am not a fraud and don't have to hold myself back from writing for fear of being seen as a fraud. I am free to write.

The next step, Step Five, involved **pairing my threat prediction statement with the prediction correction information**. Step Five is **similar to Bluetooth technology**, which is familiar to most of us.

All I know about Bluetooth is that it is a short-range wireless technology that enables us to connect electronic devices, such as cell phones, to other devices, like speakers or computers, through a process called pairing. To pair a speaker with my phone, I put both in pairing mode. When my phone 'discovers' the speaker, both devices connect and begin communicating. Similarly, Step Five involves activating the anxious emotional state associated with the threat prediction and then pairing it with the prediction correction information.

I recall feeling anxiety and the urge to withdraw and hide as I imagined myself writing. Then, I directed my attention to the contradictory experiences of accomplishment and positive feedback about what I had written. I switched my focus back and forth between these two different statements and experiences, feeling each one as I did. While doing so, I felt a shift that initially caused confusion in my brain and body. The threat of writing seemed like a dream or a mirage. What I know is that after I got back to Seattle, I started writing again. It was strange. I watched and waited for the anxiety. What once felt like eight on the Emotional Distress Scale was a one or less. I felt a measurable difference.

The transformative experience at that workshop eliminated my procrastination and changed my entire approach to psychotherapy. It set me on a path to raise awareness about emotional learning and **the transformative power of prediction corrections** to as many people as possible.

The essential process in Step Five is **the pairing process**. This involves experiencing feelings of discomfort, distress, and anxiety associated with the problem behavior you want to transform. It also activates the neural network that contains the encoded emotional learning, putting it into pairing mode. Then, you recall experiences and interactions that contain information that contradicts the predictions associated with the original emotional learning. The brain pairs the two learnings and determines that what it learned in the past is wrong (even though it feels right to you!). In this paired state, the brain unwires and opens up the neural network in which the emotional learning is encoded. It can then update that learning with new information.

Sometimes, you can activate this pairing and transformation process just by being aware of update opportunities as they present themselves, like my client Jill did.

Jill's Pairing Process

I want to tell you how Jill optimized her experiences to update her brain at some Christmas parties. Jill was seeing me to get over her debilitating social anxiety. Her family history was not uncommon: her father was emotionally absent most of her childhood, and the work of raising three children fell on her mother's shoulders. Jill described her mother as a good woman who was a demanding perfectionist, and Jill acknowledged that she understood why.

"She was like a single mom raising three kids and working part-time to make ends meet. Not easy!"

Although she identified herself as an extrovert, Jill said, *"No one would ever know that because I get very quiet and withdraw in social situations."* When she put words to the feeling beneath the anxiety and the protective mechanisms she defaults to when she is triggered, she wrote this:

If people see me as the needy person I feel I am, they will judge me as being immature, like a needy child who is a burden to her mother. They will ignore me, and I will be alone with just myself. I must never be seen as needy by anyone.

To deal with the threat of this feeling, I become anxious and quiet and withdraw like a wallflower. That way, no one will see me as the needy person I feel I am, and they won't judge and reject me.

Jill's thinking brain challenged this statement as irrational, but she acknowledged that it also felt true to her. She told me she had some holiday parties coming up, and we agreed that she would watch how this emotional learning played out in her experiences at the parties. Experiencing and thus observing the activation of a triggered emotional truth in real-time helps bring it into conscious awareness.

When we met again after the holidays, Jill told me that she paid attention to her emotional states and kept her triggering statement in mind at the parties. She described how just acknowledging her feelings and understanding their origins helped her feel more at ease. In our session, she told me that the statement still felt true, but much less so than it had when she had identified it before the holidays.

"At the first party, I let myself feel the anxiety and urge to withdraw. I reviewed the statement several times to remind myself of what was really happening. As the evening progressed, I gradually introduced myself to some people I didn't know. It felt good, and I felt proud of myself. I am not the needy person I am afraid people will see. I know that is an old feeling. I enjoyed myself and could see that engaging

and talking with people was a safe experience. People came up to me. Yeah, some slight anxiety was still there, but it didn't stop me like it used to. I just felt different."

As we discussed her experience, I suggested Jill put her party experiences into words and bring that new experience into her awareness. She wrote this:

> *Even though I learned to be afraid that people would see me as immature, like a needy child who places demands on her mother, my experiences tell me I am a positive, curious, and open adult. No one has ever rejected me for being that way—just the opposite—I like people, and people like me.*

I recommended that she use the "on one hand this... on the other this..." technique to further the updating process (I discuss this in Chapter Eleven). This is, in essence, what Jill was doing at the parties: she paired her emotional learning with her awareness of engaging with folks and enjoying her experiences of doing so. With her new statement that contradicted her old learning, Jill could continue updating her brain with Trigger-informed Mindfulness.

What Jill thought was in her way, social anxiety leading to withdrawal, was the way to free herself from its tyrannical hold on her. Her emotional learning was similar to what a harmful pathogen is to the immune system. When her brain detected her pain-infused emotional learning (a harmful pathogen), it activated withdrawal behavior to protect her from the harm it predicted she would suffer.

An Interesting Perspective: Our Brain's Emotional Immunity to Change

Our brains have an emotional immunity to change. When I initially encountered this perspective on personal change and growth, it provided an analogy that helped me understand and describe the brain's survival-based learning, predicting, and adapting process. As strange or unusual as that concept may seem, I am confident you will understand more about this comparison between our immune system's response to harmful pathogens and our brain's response to changes after you read the next section. I believe this understanding will also aid you in completing the assessments in Part II.

Our Immune System - Another Learning, Predicting, and Adapting Process

The immune system is quite a phenomenon. Like the brain, its primary purpose is to protect us from harm and ensure survival. It also operates in the background and out of awareness. Like the brain, the immune system learns, predicts, and adapts in the interests of our survival.

When the immune system detects a harmful pathogen, its memory cells 'learn' and 'remember' its characteristics—it can then recognize it in the future and neutralize or destroy it. This learning and adapting process is also predictive: **If the immune system identifies a pathogen based upon the information it acquired from prior exposure, it 'knows' what is coming and turns on the essential immuno-protective processes.**

You have an immune system, just as you have a brain. However, just as you are not your immune system, **you are not your brain**. Like your immune system, when your brain encounters an intense, emotionally harmful experience (i.e., a pathogen), it stores what it learned about that experience as an emotional memory. Like the immune system, it uses that information to screen all incoming information for harmful memories (pathogens). If, as a result of this assessment, it detects information that is crudely similar to prior learning about a harmful experience, it, like the immune system, predicts a threat and activates protective behaviors and symptoms.

An Ingenious Analogy

Robert Kegan and Lisa Laskov Lahey developed this ingenious immune system analogy and elucidated it in their book *Immunity to Change: How to Overcome It and Unlock the Potential in Yourself and Your Organization*. Their primary focus is on organizations and leadership. I have used this immune system analogy in many of my workshops to illustrate how the brain functions similarly to the immune system. I highly recommend their book to address the emotional challenges of leadership, team development, and organizational development. It focuses on the beliefs and stories (essentially emotional learnings) that reside in the subconscious.

Although it can take some effort, you can usually access your subconscious. For example, in Chapter Three, I discussed implicit procedural memory—the kind of memory associated with the many routines we perform automatically daily—with the example of using a fork. Let's say I had not acquired that knowledge and wanted to learn how to use a fork. If I ask you to help me, you could give me a step-by-step description and demonstration. It might feel a bit strange and require some effort to focus and concentrate, but you could do it. That is because the information is stored in the subconscious.

Most personal growth and self-help programs focus on techniques to change what is stored in the subconscious, and we are all familiar with them. They include affirmations, visualization, journaling, some meditative and mindfulness practices, and others. Updating the content of the subconscious has been the mainstay of self-help publications for decades. This approach can be helpful, but any changes you make require constant maintenance—they do not create the enduring transformative change we all seek. They do not involve accessing and updating what is stored in the unconscious realm of emotional learnings.

Kegan and Lahey's insights into the parallels between the immune system and behavior change processes are enlightening and beneficial. One of the most significant points that they make is **the importance of moving beyond our emphasis on technical and cognitive learning and focusing more on our innate capacities to learn, adapt, and thrive as human beings.** That focus involves emotional learning, the third dimension of learning.

Beyond the Subconscious – The Third Dimension of Mind and Memory

The etymological origin of the word 'mind' is fascinating. It originated from the Old English word *gemynd,* which referred to "memory" and dates back to before 725. Its use in other languages has the same reference to memory or remembrance.

In Chapter One, I discussed the three dimensions of learning: the first involves skills, the second encompasses information, facts, and processes, and the third is emotional learning. These three dimensions also correspond to the three layers of the mind, often depicted as an iceberg.

The tip, which is about 10% of the iceberg, is visible. That is the conscious mind. Just below the surface of the water lies the subconscious. You can become aware of it if you get close to the iceberg. However, an estimated 90% of an iceberg lies beneath the surface and is not visible. That is the unconscious. Accessing the unconscious takes effort, patience, focus, and trust. That is where your triggers lie, and that is where this book invites you to go.

I introduce Kegan and Lahey's idea about our immunity to change to reinforce the message that enduring transformation requires you to **go below the surface of your conscious mind and the shallow depths of your subconscious mind.** This is where our change efforts typically focus. The **real problem lies at the unconscious level of the mind and memory, where our emotional learnings reside. A lack of motivation or effort is not the reason our problems persist—it is our lack of knowledge and the skills to apply it.** I hope this book will help to fill that gap.

Reversing Our Brain's Emotional Immunity to Change

We all have a brain that has an emotional immunity to change when it interprets the change we want to make as one that will produce pain due to past learning. The emotional immunity then kicks in to protect itself (you), just as your immune system does when it encounters a pathogen.

Yes, it is paradoxical that our protective mechanisms also produce pain. However, this is an essential point I want to make: **There is a human** technology that can reverse your brain's emotional immunity to change, and it involves being clear about what's in the way of the change that you want to make.

What's in the Way Is the Way

I met Brenda after finishing a two-day workshop on team and patient communication for several dental practices. One part of the agenda focuses on the brain's emotional immunity to change. As I packed up my computer and finished conversations with some participants, I noticed a woman standing back, as if waiting for the others to leave. When she saw me looking at her, she approached me.

"Brian, I have a question about emotional learning. Do you have a few minutes before you leave?"

"I have lots of time. Please, what's the question?"

"I've been a dental hygienist for over twenty-five years. Although I like what I do, it creates a lot of stress for me. I get triggered when my patients don't follow my recommendations and do what I tell them to do to take care of themselves. I feel like I have let them down. So, I try harder to convince them how important it is. And that never works. I will try using some of the communication skills you presented. But I also resonated with your comment about our emotional immunity to change. I am what you call the 'anxious over-functioning professional.' However, that pattern is not limited to patients alone. I do it with my family and friends. I think it is also what caused my husband to divorce me five years ago. I've tried to change it and saw a therapist, but nothing worked. Do you think this is a way my brain has learned to protect me from painful feelings that I am unaware of? What should I do?"

"That is a good question," I responded. *"Although I don't know what you should do, I have some thoughts about what you can do that I can share with you. Before I do, I am curious about what moved you to be so open with me and ask your question?"*

Brenda looked thoughtful and said, *"I can't continue to do this. Yes, I get anxious about my patients not complying with their care plans. But it's more than that.*

I have two teenagers, and I am afraid I am losing them with my need to tell them what to do and how to be safe. My 17-year-old daughter recently told me, 'Mom, I know you love me and want me to be safe. But the more anxious you get and the more you try to control me, the more I withdraw and avoid you. It's a crazy circle we get in. Sometimes, I wish you didn't love me so much. I wish you could trust me more.'"

The anguished, tight look on Brenda's face told me she was experiencing distress just talking about her situation.

"My anxious caring is a problem and is getting in the way of the relationship I want to have with my soon-to-be adult children. It's been a problem for me for as long as I can remember. For years, my husband kept telling me he didn't need another mother in his life as he walked away from me. He would say I needed to be on drugs or have a drink. I can't do anything about that now. But I have started a new relationship, and I don't want to drive that person away with my anxious overfunctioning. What you discussed made sense to me. What should I do?"

"Brenda, when I was doing some healing work, I heard someone say, 'What's in the way is the way.'" I think what's in the way of the change you want to make is not the overfunctioning behavior itself. Recall how I mentioned these behaviors serve an essential function: they protect us from unconscious emotional pain. It may appear that anxious overfunctioning is in your way, but that behavior is showing you the way to uncover the emotional learning causing that behavior." I then directed her to the list of resources provided with the workshop handout.

And the Way Is in You

I think that you have concluded by now that one of the primary messages of this book is this: *What's in the way of any change that you want to make is not the problematic behavior or other people's behaviors or reactions. It is the unconscious emotional learning that, when triggered, drives the anxiety that causes the behavior that you want to change. Fixing the problem or symptom is a temporary solution and seldom creates the enduring transformation most people seek.*

What's in the way of transformation is the way to transformation, and that way is within you.

Summary

This chapter introduced and explored a transformative five-step human technology that optimizes the brain's survival-driven learning, prediction, and adaptation processes to eliminate emotional triggers and promote lasting personal change. It introduced an analogy that compared the body's protective immune system with the brain's emotional immunity to change.

Revisiting a Caveat

I want to reiterate something I mentioned in Chapter One. Unlike most DIY self-help processes, this process brings deep layers of unconscious emotional memories and learnings into conscious awareness. Our protective mechanisms keep those memories and their related threats at bay. If you encounter high degrees of anxiety and distress using these five steps, or if the resistance you experience in your nervous system is overwhelming, I recommend working with a therapist trained in experiential therapies and familiar with the neuroscience of implicit emotional learning and memory reconsolidation.

Now It's Your Turn

Part I addressed the first two of the four primary questions my clients ask me:

1. What is emotional learning, and how does it create triggers or emotional learnings?
2. How do emotional learnings disempower me, adversely affect my emotional well-being, and get in my way?

With the foundational understanding provided in Part I, we can now proceed to Part II, where we will apply the five-step human technology for enduring transformation. It answers the third and fourth questions my clients asked:

3. How can I uncover emotional learnings hidden within the problems I want to eliminate?
4. How can I update these emotional learnings once I become aware of them?

Now, you're ready to start transforming your emotional triggers and experience personal mastery and emotional well-being. Welcome to a 21st-century paradigm for personal empowerment and emotional well-being!

Chapter Eight
Step One:

Clarify the Problem and
the Change You Want for Yourself

When I ask my clients how I can help them, the answers are often single sentences: "I keep picking the wrong partners," "I have low self-esteem," "I have difficulty speaking up for myself," "I feel stuck in my job, but not able to move on," "I want to stop feeling so down and depressed," "My anxiety keeps me from doing things I want to do" or "I'm tired of reacting like an immature adolescent and beating myself up for it."

Then, my clients and I explore and discuss details related to the problem, including who is involved, where and when it occurs, and any related thoughts, emotions, feelings, and physical sensations that they experience. This always involves recalling specific situations in which they felt triggered, and often a discussion about when the problem first appeared. After this information gathering process, we will then clarify how they want to be different within the context in which the problem occurs.

In this chapter, you will engage in a similar two-part process:

1. **Engage in problem-focused information gathering** to clarify the problem.
2. **Clarify the specific change** that you are seeking regarding that problem.

The Devil's in the Details

In Chapter Three, I discussed how we often use idioms to describe emotional states for which we lack suitable words. For example, we often use the idiom, "I feel like I'm caught between the devil and the deep blue sea," to describe a situation in which we feel caught between choosing two adverse outcomes.

The title of this section employs an idiom to illustrate our approach to defining problems. It seems to have evolved from "God is in the details," referring to the importance of paying attention to the small details to create excellent outcomes. The devilish version suggests that even minor details can cause significant problems. Accordingly, this chapter focuses on the details related to the issue that you want to resolve and the change you desire for yourself.

Before we begin, let's face it: most of us don't engage in the kind of personal, problem-focused data collection this chapter recommends unless we have a good reason and are guided through the process. After all, who wants to spend time and effort intentionally exploring and reflecting on situations or interactions that involve emotional pain and distress unless there is some benefit to doing so?

Yes, worrying or obsessing about problems is not unusual, but that is quite different from thinking about them in an exploratory and reflective way. There are three reasons why I recommend taking the time to complete the information gathering process discussed in this chapter.

First, it provides a more detailed picture of various aspects of the problem. This information may help you become aware of cues that activate the trigger. For example, if the problem involves specific individuals, a tone of voice or the look on someone's face may be the brain's retrieval cue to trigger the threat prediction and the corresponding protective reaction.

Janeen's experience is a good example. She sought to eliminate what she described as paralyzing low self-esteem. While exploring the context in which negative emotional-thought patterns, such as "I'll never measure up" and "I'm not worthy of any recognition," gripped her, a felt sense of being scolded and shamed emerged. She recognized that the feelings were familiar to her. She could trace them back to many family interactions that involved her maternal grandparents, who lived with her family for several years during her childhood.

Second, the information that you collect often contains subtle references to the threat predictions associated with being triggered. Janeen identified a link between her self-deprecating inner talk and the threatening feelings of being scolded and shamed.

Third, reflecting on the contextual information that you gather can often help you identify the circumstances in which the emotional learning may have occurred. In Janeen's case, she could see how, in her childhood, her emotional brain learned that if she felt good about her school activities and grades, even proud of herself, and expressed that to certain family members, particularly her grandmother, she would be scolded and felt ashamed. The image she recalled was of her grandmother's harsh stare, wagging index finger, and biting tone of voice telling her, *"Janny, be careful. The Bible tells us that pride precedeth the fall."* Unbeknownst to her, she adapted to her grandmother's behavior by developing a caustic, self-directed inner dialogue. With this contextual information, she could proceed to steps two and three and create the prediction correction that would update what she had learned.

Let me provide another example to emphasize the importance of this part of Step One. During an initial phone conversation, Marianne told me that her problem was getting out of a depression she had been feeling since her father died. When we met, she expanded on the context: *"When my dad died two years ago, I was not by his side. Sadly, he died alone in a care facility. I started feeling down a few weeks after the memorial service. I can't seem to acknowledge the fact that he is gone."*

As Marianne explored her sadness and depressed state in greater depth, she discovered how the image of her father dying alone haunted her and how she felt so guilty for not being there for him. With this information, she was able to identify how depression and guilt were protecting her from feeling like she was an ungrateful, selfish, and unlovable daughter who had abandoned her father during the most vulnerable time in his life. She also recognized the origin of that feeling and the fact that she knew her dad would never have said or even inferred that. With this information, she was able to free herself from the emotional tyranny of feeling like she was an ungrateful, selfish, and unlovable daughter who had abandoned her father.

The problems that we all face do not occur in a vacuum. This chapter guides you to take a broader and deeper look at the problem, some of its history, and the context in which it occurs. With that perspective in mind, you will then clarify how you want to be different, your desired change, as the second part of Step One. This information is essential for completing Step Two, which involves identifying the emotional threat and pain that the problem protects you from experiencing, as we will explore in Chapter Nine.

The First and Second Parts of Step One: Clarifying the Problem and the Desired Change

The following nine problem statements are the outcomes of clients' recalling scenes or experiences in which they felt triggered and thus could access information about the context. As they recall the scene, I listen for information about the context and will often ask clarifying questions depending on the problem. I don't expect you to answer the questions below, as I have provided some for your assessment in another section in this chapter. Consider these questions as a warm-up for the process you will be undertaking.

- What is my client doing that they don't want to do, and what do they want to do instead?
  - This information relates to problematic behavior patterns and the desired difference.
- What is my client telling herself about herself and the world around her that is in the way of doing what she desires to do?
  - This information pertains to self-deprecating emotional-thought patterns.
- What is my client reporting about how emotional states, such as anxiety and depression, inhibit her from moving forward with her life?

- o This information relates to inhibitory emotional state patterns of anxiety and depression and looks to assess what my client would be doing if she were not experiencing these emotional states.
- Who is involved in the problem?
  - o Does the problem involve family members, friends, co-workers, relationship partners, etc.?
- Are any emotions, feelings, or physical sensations associated with the triggered experience?
- Recalling a triggered experience is usually accompanied by some feelings of anxiety, dread, or fear, which is the brain's early warning system of a threat. These emotions are often accompanied by physical sensations in the area of the body from the neck to the lower abdomen. Clients have described these sensations as a tight grip on or lump in the throat, a hollow emptiness in the solar plexus, a surge of heat or a collapsing feeling in the chest, or a vise gripping the shoulders and upper body.
- Are there any indications of what the client feels will happen if she does not do the problematic behavior?
  - o Without any awareness of doing so, clients often make subtle references to the threat of what will happen if they don't engage in the emotionally mandated protective behavior.
- Is the problem context-specific or generalized to different areas of the client's life?
  - o This information relates to where and when the problem occurs and can help clarify the threat prediction and correction statements. Clients often report that the problem occurs only in specific settings, such as business meetings or family gatherings.
- Is there any sensory information included in the problem description?
  - o Are there any specific sights, sounds, or scents that the client references in their context description?
- What change do my clients want for themselves?

○ Clarifying the desired change is not as easy as the words imply. Sometimes, we become so accustomed to being stuck that imagining something different can be a challenge. It can also be challenging to imagine yourself changing without others changing as well.

You will reflect on similar questions when you complete your problem assessment later in this chapter. Even if you have already written down the problem, I suggest using the questions in that section as a filter to gather more information.

Nine Examples of Step One

With the questions above in mind, let's examine some of the problems my clients sought to eliminate and the changes they desired. As you read these, try to identify the threat that may be embedded within each person's statement.

1. **Pauline**
   Problem: *I often get nervous and take control of discussions when people share stories about things they have done. I hate feeling like I have to keep up with them, but that is what it feels like, and if I don't jump in, I feel like I will be ignored. I'd rather be calm and allow the conversations to flow, but that's hard to do when I get that anxious feeling. I have to jump in.*
   Desired Change:
   I want to stay calm and curious with my friends and people at work when they talk about their different experiences.

2. **Simone**
   Problem: *I'm tired of pretending everything is okay between my husband and me. And I don't want to admit it to myself, but I feel depressed. I've been playing this game for years, and I'm at a breaking point, but if I talk to him about how I feel, he will be so hurt that it will damage him forever, and I feel it will be my fault if he is hurt. Somehow, this is how I think my mother felt with my dad.*

Desired Change:

I have imagined myself talking with Jeremy about how depressed and tired I feel, and that I need him to step up and even recommend counseling for us. I want to make that image a reality and have the conversation I keep avoiding. It is the conversation I know my mother never had with my dad, and it took a big toll on her.

3. **Gary**

Problem: *I am tired of being with partners who are bad for me. It feels really good and intense to start. After a few months, things get crazy for me. I feel like I have to be very careful about what I say and can never do the right things to make her happy. Sometimes, it feels like it all works well, and then she's unhappy, angry, or disappointed, and I feel it is my fault. I go back and forth between feeling rejected and becoming sheepish, to feeling like I can't live without her, and am desperate for her approval and love. The ups and downs are crazy, and the relationship usually ends in a big storm.*

Desired Change: *I want to trust that I can be in a stable, close relationship in which I feel I can be open about what I am feeling without feeling like I can never do anything right because I never know what right is or it is constantly changing.*

4. **Nancy**

Problem: *I always feel depressed after I visit my family, and it takes about a week or so to get out of it. As a result, I make up lots of excuses as to why I can't visit them as often as they want me to. I think it is my mother's attitude about life. I don't know how my dad has done it all these years. She is just so pessimistic and scared all the time. Sometimes, I want to shake and tell her to snap out of it. But instead, I do what I did as a kid. I pretend to go along with how bad things are and all the negative things she says my aunt and uncle do. I don't know if depression is contagious, but when I leave home, I feel like I caught it from her.*

Desired Change: *It is important to me that I stop pretending when I am with my family. I want to tell my mother that I see the world differently from her and that it is okay for her and me to be that way.*

I want to let her know I love her and that it makes me sad that she sees the world that way.

5. **Leo**

   Problem: *I feel like I am constantly being judged, like someone in the defendant's chair in a courtroom. I must be on the lookout to ensure I'm not guilty of doing something wrong. It's there in all my significant relationships, except for a few close friends who accept me and know my struggles. It feels like a harsh and critical judge is waiting to banish me.*

   Desired Change: *I want to be free of the anxiety and threat of being judged for doing something wrong. If I make a mistake, I want to know and feel I will be okay and can deal with it.*

6. **Manny**

   Problem: *I want a closer relationship with my adult children, but I don't want them to feel like they have to take care of me. So, I avoid discussing it with them and drop little hints instead, hoping they get the picture. It's what my wife did with her mother, and I think the stress killed her.*

   Desired Change: *The only change I want is to be able to talk with my adult children about how I feel and discuss my concerns about how they feel. I know they know how their mom felt trapped by her mother, and I don't want them to feel the same way.*

7. **William**

   Problem: *I'm tired of doing everything people want me to do. Starting with my wife. then my boss. Then my parents. Feels like for my whole life. I want them to get off my back. But I have to keep up the front. So much depends on me. What are my options? None. So, yeah, I'd like to tell everyone to f#@k off, but that would not be good. I feel stuck with no way out.*

   Desired Change: *The only change I want is to be able to tell people what I can and can't do when they ask. I want to negotiate different responsibilities with my boss and set some limits with my wife.*

8. **Cyrus**

Problem: *I'm on heart meds and blood pressure medication. I'm overweight and have a hard time sleeping. Both my wife and my doctor tell me I have to slow down. When I tried that, I felt like I was bored. It felt restless, tense, and uncomfortable. My doctor said it was anxiety and suggested I take a small dose of an anti-anxiety med to see if it helped. No way. I'm on enough meds. That's when my wife suggested I talk to somebody like you.*

Desired Change: *I want to slow down and hire a manager-type person who can do the running around I have to do. The business can afford it, and I can handle the books, but the daily grind is getting to me. That's hard to admit because I have always worked a lot.*

9. **Sally**

Problem: *I know I need to be a better leader with my team. That means being clear and precise in my communication, particularly when they are not following through with what needs to be done to provide the best care for our patients. However, just the thought of being clear stops me in my tracks. They tell me they want more direction, but I'd rather discuss what we need to do in team meetings than discuss it with them individually. I also know from talking with my colleagues that I'm not alone. But that doesn't change what I do.*

Desired Change: *I want to be clear, direct, and respectful in my communication and relationships with my team members. I also want to calmly follow up with them on my requests.*

I am providing these examples to give you some perspective on how clients have clarified their problems and the desired change they each wanted. You may have sensed the threats embedded within some of their statements, as well as what each person wanted to be different. Consider Sally's reference to "*...just the thought of being clear stops me in my tracks*" or Simone's "*...he will be so hurt that it will damage him forever and it will be my fault.*" Consider the threat predictions in Leo having "*...to ensure I'm not guilty of doing something wrong,*" and Pauline's "I feel like I will be ignored."

Further, note what some of them said they wanted to do differently. For example, Pauline's reference to *"I want to stay calm and curious with my friends and colleagues when they talk about their different experiences,"* and Sally's *"I want to be clear, direct, and respectful in my communication and relationships with my team members. I also want to follow up with them on my requests calmly."*

Suzanne's Problem and Her Desired Change

Before we move on to your assessment of the problem and your desired change, I want to bring you up to date on Suzanne's journey to free herself from the emotional learning associated with the threat of expressing herself. Recall that we last discussed Suzanne at the end of Chapter Six; she was in her thirties. I described and illustrated how she (her brain) is triggered under certain circumstances. Although she knows the behavior she wants to change, she is unaware of the threat prediction that causes the behavior.

Suzanne described her problem this way: *I get triggered when people ask me for ideas about what I'd like to do or my thoughts about what they want us all to do; it's like I freeze up. It also happens when I want to express what I want. My throat tightens up, and I feel blank for a moment. It feels like I don't have a voice. It happens at work. My manager values my opinion and repeatedly asks me what is holding me back. I hate that it is happening with my boyfriend because the last guy I liked got tired of always having to guess what I wanted. I can't seem to tell people what I want or my ideas. It's so immature. It feels like there is a wall in me that I keep bumping up against.*

As Suzanne thought about the many situations in which she experienced needing to withdraw, she concluded that the change she most desired was *"...to feel free to express myself and my thoughts and preferences without the fear of being shamed and rejected. I want to recognize that people may not always agree with me and feel they have the same freedom I do."*

Suzanne took **a few days to observe herself interacting** with her boyfriend, friends, and coworkers, keeping her written statement of the problem and desired change in mind. As a result, she revised her Desired Change to read as follows: *I want to express myself and my thoughts and preferences, recognize that people may not always agree with me, and know that they have the same freedom I do.*

The value of this **brief observation process** lies in its often providing insights into the trigger's emotional origins. Although Suzanne was aware of her father's verbally abusive language and behavior, she had never looked at it through the lens of emotional learning. Accordingly, it often happens that when people engage in this observation behavior, they gain a glimpse of both the threat prediction and the protective behavior that shields them from that threat. This happened for Suzanne, and we will follow up with her as she completes Step Two in Chapter Nine.

Now It's Your Turn

Part One: Clarify the Problem

As I mentioned earlier in this chapter, we often get caught up in worrying about our problems, but few of us think about the details of what that problem involves, let alone write about it. So, this first part of Phase One can be an interesting challenge. You may feel the urge to override information as it comes up because it is uncomfortable, or ignore details that emerge because they don't seem relevant. That is quite natural and to be expected. You've heard this said many times: Trust the process.

This section includes questions that facilitate your assessment process. They are based upon the questions that you read earlier, but adapted to assist you in doing this in a self-directed way. First, you will recall a specific situation or interaction in which the problem occurs. This recall process will trigger the anxious and uncomfortable feelings your brain associates with the interaction or situation. Switching from experiencing the triggered experience to observing and writing about it can be a challenging task. To facilitate this process, I suggest using your cellphone's recorder to discuss the problem and its context as you explore the following questions. Then, listen to it and write down what you recorded. If recording is not possible, I recommend another option. You can ask someone whom you trust to assist by sitting with you and asking questions. (Tell that person you need a quiet listening witness who will read the questions to you and write down the answers. There is no need to fix you or help you solve it.) If you use this option, ask them to change the pronoun in the questions from "I to "you" and the verbs from "am" to "are" where applicable.

> - What do I feel as I recall this scene? Are there uncomfortable emotions, feelings, or physical sensations I recognize?
> - Does anything stand out to me as I recall the scene? For example, the look on people's faces, tones of voice, and spoken words.
> - What am I telling myself about the situation? Do any negative self-directed thoughts and beliefs emerge within me?
> - Who is involved in the scene? What do I feel they will do if I do what I want to do?
> - How do I want to feel and think about myself that I cannot let myself feel or think?
> - How is this problem an issue for me? What distress does it cause me?

As I mentioned, you may feel resistance regardless of how you complete this problem assessment. That is a good sign, as it means your exploration is triggering emotional information related to the problem.

Your initial responses may be rambling, but rest assured, you have become aware of some important information. If you used a recording device, listen to it with an open mind and write down what you recorded.

Part Two: Clarify the Change You Want for Yourself

Part Two of Step One involves clearly stating what you want to be different regarding the problem you have just clarified. This reflection only involves what you want to be different for yourself. It is not unusual for us to wish that others would change. For example, imagine Suzanne saying she will express herself only when everyone in her life guarantees that they will never question her stated preferences or be curious about what she wants— asking others to change so that we are comfortable and trigger-free is, as we all know, a fruitless and frustrating fantasy. Therefore, give yourself some time and grace as you clearly state the change that you want for yourself.

To complete this assessment, it can be helpful to imagine what you want to do that the problem inhibits and prevents you from doing. Reflect on the statement of the problem you developed. Can you clarify what the identified problem prevents you from doing in one or two sentences? Here are some prompting questions to assist with this clarification process. It may also help to review the examples presented in this chapter.

Does the difference you want to create involve:
- Expressing yourself and communicating with others, and if so, what is it you want to communicate?
- Engaging in specific activities that your protective behavior inhibits you from doing?
  ◦ Examples might include advancing your education or taking classes in topics of interest, maintaining a self-care program, or following through on an important personal project.
- Defining the positive way that you want to manage your experience of the trigger-activating behavior of others?
- Experiencing freedom from the limitations associated with depression and anxiety. If that is the case, what will you do with your new-found freedom?
- Reducing and eliminating the distracting and self-limiting experience of negative emotional-thought patterns. If this is the case, what would you be doing that those patterns prevent you from doing?

Many clients have found it valuable to spend a few days or even a week reflecting on and, if possible, observing what they wrote to validate it. Although not essential, it can be helpful to do this as it can support further clarification and validation of what you have written.

Summary

This chapter focused on the initial step in this five-step transformational process: clarifying the problem and the specific change one desires. It emphasizes the importance of detailed, reflective exploration of the problem context, associated emotions, and triggers to better understand the underlying issues and set clear goals for change.

What is the Threat That Your Brain Needs to Protect You From?

The next Step in our Five-step process involves identifying the threat that your survival-biased brain predicts, which makes experiencing the difference that you just clarified very difficult, or, in most cases, impossible. Before we move on to Step Two, I want to reiterate a message that appears frequently throughout this book:

> *Your emotional brain learned something in the past that predicts an imminent threat when that learning is triggered in the present, but you don't know what that learning is! When that learning is triggered, the brain turns on the threat alarm of anxiety and activates protective behaviors. Your brain is doing its evolutionary job to ensure your survival. That learning is outdated and needs to be updated. However, you can't update something if you are unaware of what it is.*

That is the focus of Step Two in Chapter Nine.

Chapter Nine
Steps Two and Three:
Discover, Clarify, and Validate the Threat Prediction and Your Protective Behavior

It's natural to want to fix a problem or change something that is causing distress and preventing us from living the life that we want to live, the relationships that we want to enjoy, and the success that we want to experience. This is the focus of most change efforts: We have identified a problem and want to do something about it, or we learn to live with it and its associated distress.

Given that you have read this far, I think it is clear to you that this book presents a different approach to addressing problems, as well as promoting personal change and growth. I have referred to this as making your brain right by making it wrong using a five-step human technology for enduring transformation. In Chapter Seven, I compared our brain's threat prediction and protective processes to our body's immune system. I described how **our brains have an emotional immunity to change when the brain detects that the desired change is a threat based on past experiences**.

This chapter involves Steps Two and Three of our journey to become trigger-free.

Step Two focuses on **identifying the pain-infused emotional learnings that serve as triggers and the protective behavior patterns** that your brain has developed and uses to protect you from this threat.

Step Three invites you to **observe and validate what you discover**. As you observe yourself in this way, you may begin to notice a tiny gap between the stimulus and your brain's response to it. You may also change what you wrote based on your observations.

Before we put on our emotional hard hats to explore the emotional brain's deep strata, I'd like to address a question many clients have asked me: *"Are there positive triggers?"* My answer comes from my experiences; you may have a different response. I call them sparks.

Are There Positive Triggers?

We have come to associate the term 'trigger' and the experience of being triggered with adverse emotional reactions and distress. Given its historical association with painful emotional experiences and trauma, that is understandable.

However, I suggest that we also have many positive triggers—emotional learnings that enable us to experience love, joy, curiosity, awe, and wonder. We want to celebrate experiences of feeling resilient, trusting in our wisdom, and speaking our truth. We want to strengthen emotional learnings that support us as we move forward to achieve our dreams, delight in our successes, and rebound from our disappointments. You might recognize these positive triggers as the feeling of a comforting hug, the warm and affectionate smile of a loving partner, the laughter of friends delighting in just being together, or a sense of pride and accomplishment after completing an important project. I think of these **experiences as sparks**, not triggers.

The best experiences I have of sparks are watching the faces and looking into the eyes of babies and young children. There, I see so much potential, curiosity, and openness. I feel a spark of awe in the face of a beautiful mystery. I wonder what these little ones experience that I have long forgotten, yet still remember unconsciously and feel when I look at them. I think that these experiences are sparks that help us remember the beauty, wonder, and mystery of being alive. I believe we all seek to remember these **sparks of life** and are often prevented from doing so by layers of pain-infused triggers.

I am bringing this to your attention because I have found, both personally and professionally, that we tend to focus more on our negative and painful experiences than on our positive and pleasurable ones. Thus, from a neuroscience standpoint, we are strengthening experiences (memories) of what we don't want and forgetting to strengthen what we do want. I believe that we all need to strengthen positive memories that we can use to update and eliminate the negative emotional learnings that cause us so much distress.

So, my answer to that question is YES! **We do have positive triggers, which I call sparks**, and in Chapter Ten, I recommend a specific three-part process I call the SFT approach to establish and strengthen sparks (memories of pleasant experiences). The specific steps for the SFT method are included in Section #2 of the Appendix. With that said, let us continue our exploration and discovery work.

Implicit Emotional Learning is the Real Problem

In Chapter One, I discussed how triggers are implicit emotional learnings associated with intense, painful emotional experiences. We spend enormous amounts of emotional and mental energy, and money, trying to manage and overcome these threats and restore ourselves after they are triggered. I hope that I have demonstrated that this approach, although beneficial, leads to only short-term relief. The cause of the problem you want to eliminate is the implicit emotional learning that generates the threat prediction. Unless that learning is brought to your conscious awareness and updated, it will continue to control aspects of your life and create distress.

At the end of Chapter Seven, I mentioned the phrase, 'What's in the way is the way.' What you think is in your way is the problem you identified in Chapter Eight. However, that **problem points the way to what's really in the way**.

This chapter focuses on how we can **discover, clarify, and validate the real problem**. Remember, this process is not about dwelling on the negative or looking for who is to blame. Those are, after all, protective mechanisms. **The 21st-century approach is about engaging with the problem, not counteracting it.**

The Experience of the Paradigm Shift

In the Introduction, I discussed how learning about emotional learning, the brain's predictive and adaptive process, and the neuroscience of enduring transformation was a paradigm shift for me, both personally and professionally. It was a shift from the counteractive paradigm for coping with problems and symptoms to one that involved engaging and exploring them to become aware of the emotional learnings that were causing them. I also commented that I still relapse into that counteractive approach on occasion.

I'm bringing this to your attention again because I am fairly certain you will feel yourself counteracting what you may discover. That might show up as cognitive resistance that might minimize or negate what you discover, or emotions and physical sensations that 'tell' you to push away what emerges. You may find yourself feeling selfish or guilty for focusing on yourself, and judging yourself for even allowing yourself to become aware of your emotional learning.

When this happens, your brain is doing its counteractive protective process. Therefore, expect to experience what we commonly refer to as resistance. When you notice any tendency to override or overcome what may arise with you, make note of that observation. That is the counteractive process. Instead, simply observe what is happening and continue to engage in discovering what you learned that you didn't know you learned. Be curious about what lies within you.

I think Ralph Waldo Emerson described this outcome of this exploration well when he said, "*What lies behind us and what lies before us are tiny matters compared to what lies within us.*"

Suzanne Understands Why She Must Do What She Does

I want to use the nine examples of problem and desired change statements from the previous chapter to illustrate Step Two. First, let's continue Suzanne's story by sharing the outcome of her threat discovery process.

Recall from Chapter Eight that Suzanne described her problematic behavior this way: *I get triggered when people ask me for ideas about what I'd like to do or my thoughts about what they want us all to do; it's like I freeze up. My throat tightens up, and I feel blank for a moment. It feels like I don't have a voice. It happens at work. My manager values my opinion and repeatedly asks me what is holding me back. I hate that it is happening with my boyfriend because the last guy I liked got tired of always having to guess what I wanted. I can't seem to tell people what I want or my ideas. It's so immature. It feels like there is a wall in me I keep bumping up against.*

Her Desired Change read like this: *I want to feel free to express myself and my thoughts and preferences, recognize that people may not always agree with me, and know that they have the same freedom I do.*

Although she was aware of her father's toxic behavior from her previous psychotherapy, she had never looked at it through the lens of emotional learning. In terms of her brain's emotional immunity to change, expressing herself and asking for what she wants is a harmful pathogen.

Through this new lens, she clarified the threat prediction and her protective behavior pattern. Before you read what she wrote, imagine that Suzanne is a close friend who has been sharing her journey of discovery with you. You are sitting with her as she tells you that she now understands why, despite all your encouragement and support, and her attempts at change, she still struggles to express herself. She would like to share this awareness with you. Reflect on the following questions as she shares what she discovered.

> What is your emotional reaction?
>
> What does your thinking brain want to do?
>
> Do you feel like countering her threat prediction with statements of affirmation and support?
>
> What is the hardest part for you to take in as she communicates what she discovers?

Suzanne's Threat Prediction:

If I speak up and ask for what I want, or use my voice to express my ideas or opinions, then people will shame and reject me, just like my father did. I will not matter to anyone and will be left alone without anyone to be with.

Her Protective Behavior:

The way I deal with this feeling is to become anxious and withdraw into silence or just go along with what is happening. I avoid telling people what I want and, if I can, avoid speaking up at work and sharing my ideas. If I have to do that at work, I will become anxious and worry that someone will call me out, and I will feel horrible shame. I must never express myself; it is just too dangerous.

Did you feel uncomfortable with what she shared with you? Perhaps you felt and thought what many of us experience when threat predictions are brought into the light of our conscious awareness. It's what I discussed in Chapter Three about the irrational logic of the emotional brain. Suzanne's threat prediction is completely logical based on what her emotional brain learned. It is also irrational, and our thinking brain struggles with that. You may have felt like countering her statements.

I bring this to your attention because you will likely experience this when you discover and clarify the threat prediction that lies beneath your protective behavior. You may also experience this when reading the nine examples of threat prediction and protection statements in this chapter.

I have integrated Suzanne's threat prediction and protection statements into the illustration presented in Illustration 9.1. It builds on the prior illustrations that I used to visually portray Suzanne's experience and transformational journey.

Illustration 9.1 – Suzanne's Brain in Protection Mode

The numbers in the illustration correspond with the explanations below.

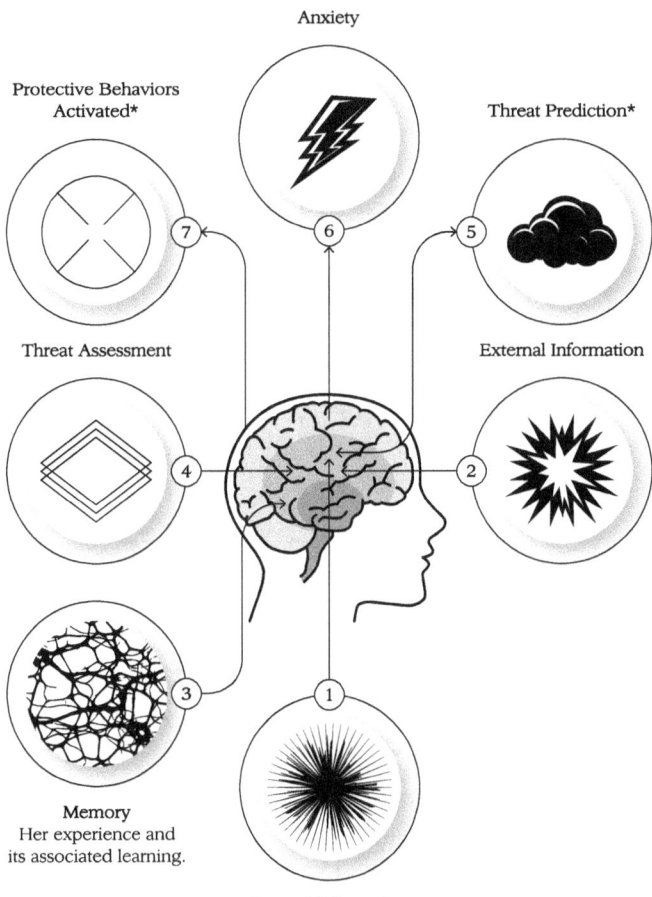

* *Threat Prediction*
If I speak up and ask for what I want or use my voice to express my ideas or opinions, then people will shame and reject me like my father did. I will not matter to anyone and will be left alone without anyone to be with. I must never express myself; it is just too dangerous.

* *Protective Behaviors Activated*
II must withdraw into silence or just go along with what is happening. I avoid telling people what I want and, if I can, avoid speaking up at work and sharing my ideas. If I have to do that at work, I will become anxious and worry that someone will call me out, and I will feel horrible shame. I must never express myself; it is just too dangerous.

Suzanne's brain perceives (1) internal or (2) external stimuli and does its (4) threat assessment using its past learnings (3) as input. That assessment process detects and triggers the emotional learning (3) that involves past suffering. It then (5) predicts an imminent future experience of suffering based on that learning and turns on the alarm signal of anxiety (6). Suzanne is triggered. That signal activates her protective behaviors of withdrawal and accommodation (7). This all happens in fractions of a second!

The title of one of the sections in Chapter Five was "If the Brain Predicts a Threat, It Must Protect from the Threat." This means that when pain-infused emotional learnings are triggered, it is imperative that the brain issue a protection command, just like your immune system must stop invasive pathogens. After all, as far as your brain is concerned, your survival is at stake! As I mentioned in Chapters Five and Six, you will notice the words 'must' and 'have to' in the examples below.

Nine Examples of Threat Prediction and Protection Statements

Chapter Eight contained nine examples of client statements of problems and their desired changes. This section builds on those examples and presents their correlated threat predictions and protective behaviors. They were generated by exploring the emotional strata and feelings underlying the problems they sought to eliminate.

You will notice that some of these statements refer to the situation or circumstances in which the learning may have happened. Memories often emerge when people explore and uncover the meaning of the uncomfortable emotional state associated with the problematic behavior they want to change. I encourage them to write down these memories as they can be beneficial for developing prediction corrections (Step Four in Chapter Ten).

These examples provide only the desired change, the threat prediction, and the protective behavior. You can refer back to the problem statements in Chapter Eight if you want to reread the problems.

1. **Pauline**

   Desired Change:

   I want to be able to stay calm and curious with my friends and people at work when they are talking about their different experiences.

   Threat Prediction:

   If people are talking about their activities and what they are doing as a family, I will be ignored and become invisible, just like what happened in Middle School when all the kids talked about their vacations and what their families were doing. I felt so left out that I just withdrew because I felt like I wasn't good enough. That all changed in high school because my mom started working. We had more money and did more things. That's when I started to feel like I had to jump in, just like today, or I will feel the same awful feelings I felt back then.

   Protective Behavior:

   I must make sure that people know that I am as good as them. When I feel left out, I get anxious and jump in with comments about what is happening in my life. Sometimes, I exaggerate things, so people know that we're doing okay.

2. **Simone**

   Desired Change:

   I have imagined myself talking with Jeremy about how depressed and tired I feel and that I need him to step up and even recommend counseling for us. I want to make that image a reality and have the conversation that I keep avoiding. It is the conversation I know my mother never had with my dad, and it took a big toll on her.

   Threat Prediction:

   If I do what my mother never did, I will cause great harm to Jeremy, and it will be my fault. But if I don't, I will continue down the road of depression and resentment. I don't know how I'll manage when the kids go to college; they keep me busy and active. But after they leave, my life will be empty, just like my mother's. But if I talk with him and he falls apart, then I am stuck with him, which feels unbearable. Then, I would need to get a divorce, and my mother would feel like she wasted her life, and it would be my fault she felt that way. That would make me a very selfish person who doesn't deserve love.

Protective Behavior:

I must do what my mother did and put up with what is happening because if I don't, she will feel that her marriage and life were a waste, and I will feel like a selfish, uncaring person. The way I deal with this feeling is to pretend everything is going well. I would rather be depressed and pretend I am happy than hurt my mother by deciding to take care of myself and living the life that is truly me.

3. **Gary**

Desired Change:

I want to trust that I can be in a stable, close relationship in which I feel I can be open about what I am feeling without feeling like I can never do anything right because I never know what right is or it is constantly changing.

Threat Prediction:

If I get too close to someone and start to care for them and let them care for me, the other shoe will always drop, and they will switch on me and reject me. It will be just like it was at home with my mother. I was either her favorite or I was ignored, like I didn't matter. I never knew which mother would show up. I know how to survive ups and downs, but stability is unpredictable and actually scary.

Protective Behavior:

I must choose partners who feel intense at first and who then become emotionally unpredictable because then I know what to do when the other shoe drops because it always does. That way, I don't have to live in dread waiting for the other shoe to drop.

4. **Nancy**

Desired Change:

It is important to me that I stop pretending when I am with my family. I need to tell my mother that I see the world differently from her and that it is okay for me to be that way. I want to let her know I love her and that it makes me sad for her that she sees the world as she does, and that I understand why she does.

Threat Prediction:

To belong to the family, everyone must go along with mom and not upset her by disagreeing with her. If I speak up for myself and tell her that I see the world differently, I won't belong anymore and will be left out of family events, even though I don't want to go to most of them anyway. I'd rather go along with everyone than risk not belonging to the family.

Protective Behavior:

I deal with this uncomfortable feeling by hiding what is really going on for me and doing what everyone else does. We start drinking as soon as we all get together. It seems there's always a reason to have a drink, and my family finds lots of reasons.

5. **Leo**

   Desired Change:

   I want to be free of the anxiety and threat of being banished if I make a mistake. If I make a mistake, I want to know I can deal with it.

   Threat Prediction:

   If I am found guilty of doing something wrong, I will be punished by being ignored and sent into exile, where I will be all alone. I must not be found guilty of doing something wrong, so I must always do things perfectly or find a way of pleasing people so they won't find me guilty.

   Protective Behavior:

   I have to do everything I can to make sure I am never found guilty of making a mistake, and if I am, I must withdraw into silence and become invisible, so I am never banished.

6. **Manny**

   Desired Change:

   The only change I want is to be able to talk with them about how I feel and discuss my concerns about how they feel. I know they know how their mom felt trapped by her mother, and I don't want them to feel the same way.

Threat Prediction:

If I talk about what I want in my relationships with Jackson and Jacqui, I feel they will feel I need them to take care of me. I will then be a burden like my mother-in-law, Mary, was for many years to my wife, Sue. They will then be angry at me for being so dependent on them, like Sue felt. I will not let them be angry with me for trapping them, like Sue was trapped by her mother.

Protective Behavior:

The way I deal with this threat is to give hints about what I would like in my relationship with them. I avoid discussing my desire to spend more time with them because I will be a terrible burden to them.

7. **William**

Desired Change:

The only change I want is to be able to tell people what I can and can't do when they ask. I want to negotiate different responsibilities with my boss and also set some limits with my wife.

Threat Prediction:

If I don't do what important people in my life ask me to do, they will blame me for their unhappiness, and it will be my fault that their lives will be ruined. I know this sounds crazy, and I know it's not true, but it feels so true. I must do what I am asked to do, or else I will suffer the pain of making my family, my parents, and my boss unhappy and disappointed in me. I will be an irresponsible, undependable person, just like my grandfather. I will be rejected and ignored. People will cut me out of their lives and never let me back.

Protective Behavior:

I must not risk feeling the pain of being rejected and ignored for being irresponsible and undependable, and I will do what it takes to make sure that never happens. There are many stories about the suffering that my grandfather's sinful and irresponsible behavior caused the family and the shame he brought on everyone. I must make sure they never say those things about me and cut me out like they did to him.

8. **Cyrus**

Desired Change:

I want to slow down and hire a manager-type person who can do the running around I have to do. The business can afford it, and I can handle the books, but the daily grind is getting to me. That's hard to admit because I have always worked a lot.

Threat Prediction:

If I free myself from my daily grind and take time for myself, I will be harshly punished, just like my father did if I wasn't always busy doing something. I know he's gone, but the feeling that I will be beaten is still there. I just didn't know how strong it was. He would scream that an idle mind is the devil's workshop as he whipped me with his belt. I must make sure I don't get whipped again.

Protective Behavior:

To make sure I don't feel the terror I used to feel when my father beat me, I must always keep myself busy doing something productive. I can't let myself slow down or else I will be severely punished.

9. **Sally**

Desired Change:

I want to be clear, direct, and respectful in my relationships with my team members. I also want to calmly follow up with them on my requests.

Threat Prediction:

If I am clear, direct, and even respectful in my communication with my team members, they will see me as a bully who doesn't care about their feelings. Then they will leave me, and my practice will fail, and I will fail. As I think about this threat, I can feel it. But I also see where I learned this. The rule in my family was to never ask for what you want because anybody who did was criticized for acting like they were more important than anybody else and accused of being a demanding brat who didn't care for others.

Protective Behavior:

I protect myself from being seen as a bully who doesn't care for people by becoming anxious and avoiding the important conversations I need to have. I hide behind the word 'we' and never say 'I' because it is uncomfortable. I must never clearly ask for what I want from them.

Now It's Your Turn

This discovery process requires patience and a willingness to let your feelings speak their truth. For most of us, that is a challenging thing to do. Think about Ashley and the anxiety she feels when she is helping her daughter learn the ABCs, my writing procrastination, Derrick and his anxious withdrawal, or the nine examples in the previous section.

When you work with a therapist to discover and bring unconscious learning into conscious awareness, she will attend to your words and emotions and facilitate the exploration and clarification process. However, there are some approaches you can take to undertake your own discovery work.

Step #2 - Discover and Clarify Your Unique Threat Prediction and Protective Behavior

Keep this in mind as you enter into this activity: What *you are bringing into your window of awareness is a prediction that your brain is making about a threat that it has detected in the present based on the memory of an experience, a painful one.* Let me offer a common example of how we often refer to our awareness of these threats.

Mommy and Daddy Issues

You have probably heard references to **'daddy issues'** or **'mommy issues.'** For example, a friend might become upset with you and go quiet during a conversation. Later, she might apologize and tell you, "It's just my daddy issues." Statements like this are often accompanied by mild laughter or a response like, "Yeah, I know what you mean," or "No problem." Or you might hear another friend tell you that he has 'mommy issues' because of the way his dominant mother ruled the roost with an iron hand.

However, **a threat prediction is hidden within these references** to mommy and daddy issues. For example, if your 'daddy issue' friend could identify the threat prediction it refers to, it might go something like this: *If I disappoint you, then you will get angry with me and criticize me, just like my dad did when I disappointed him. When that happened to me, I would close down and go quiet, just like I did with you a few minutes ago.* You might counter your friend's statement with an affirmation of the friendship and assurances that you weren't disappointed, perhaps with the hope that she will change her thinking. Your friend with 'mommy issues' may have learned this: *If I don't make you feel happy, then you will close me out and ignore me, just like my mother did when she was not happy with me.* In both examples, nothing will change until your friend updates the threat-infused emotional learnings that caused their reactions.

I discuss these examples to illustrate how much we might already know about the causes of our problematic behavior patterns, but have never examined them through the lens of the emotional learning and threat prediction process. Becoming trigger-free involves clarifying and documenting what the brain predicts will happen to you if you don't follow its emotional mandate for protection and then updating those threats with new information.

Clarify the Threat Prediction

In Chapter Five, I discussed how we utilize the brain's predictive process to create desired outcomes or acquire new knowledge, and introduced a simple prediction logic statement to illustrate this: If this (the action I will perform), then this (the outcome I will obtain). Like implicit procedural memory, this is a subconscious process. For example, if I asked you to describe how you used your brain's predictive process to buy groceries, you'd probably give me a very quizzical look.

However, if we took the time, you and I could identify the predictive process that you used to complete that task. Your brain uses the same prediction process in its unconscious threat assessment of incoming information. I recommend using the format presented in the box below to articulate the threat prediction.

> The format of the statement of the unconscious threat prediction process follows the "if this....then this . . ." format.
>
> *If . . . . (the action I want to do, or something happens that triggers me) then . . . . (the prediction of what your emotional learning says will happen to you.)*
>
> Because the emotional brain is logical, you can construct a statement about the meaning of the feeling you don't want to feel. Just don't expect that statement to be rational! After all, it is an old learning acquired under emotionally intense circumstances without any awareness of what you were learning.
>
> To do this exercise, you need to trigger the protective behavior and let yourself feel the discomfort and anxiety that accompany it. One of the most effective ways to do this is to recall a memory in which you were triggered.

Here are two more examples from clients who used this process to identify the underlying meaning of feelings that caused the problems they wanted to change. I have also included the changes they wanted for themselves and the problematic behaviors they used to protect themselves from the identified threat.

Milly is a 42-year-old woman who wants to decrease her anxious overfunctioning with her aging parents. To trigger herself, she recalled experiences of them calling her and the anxiety that she felt while on the phone with them as they made demands.

Desired Change:
I want to discuss with my aging parents what I can do for them, and how I am not always available when they need me. I want to work out a way to meet their needs while still allowing me to have a life of my own, like a problem-solving discussion.

Threat Prediction:

This feeling tells me that if I say no to my parents' constant demands for help and establish boundaries with them, then they will be angry with me and reject me, just as I feel they did when I was a child, when they were both busy with work.

Protective Behavior:

I deal with this feeling by doing whatever they ask, even if it means I do not have a life of my own. I use alcohol to ease my anxiety and get angry at myself for not talking to them about my concerns. I must do what they ask and avoid the risk of being rejected, as I felt I was when I was a child.

Geraldine is a 59-year-old grandmother with a lifelong pattern of anxious overfunctioning and controlling behavior. Her primary problem involved serious depressive symptoms. She was so immobilized that she had contemplated taking her life. To trigger herself, she brought up memories of her adult children telling her to relax and that they didn't need her to do everything like she used to.

Desired Change:

I want to be more available and enjoy spending time with my adult children and grandchildren.

Threat Prediction:

If I am not useful and can't help the people important to me, my life doesn't mean anything, and I might as well not be here. I must be useful by helping those important to me, even when they don't want me to, because if I'm not, things will fall apart, and it will be my fault. I have felt that way since I was seven years old, when my mother got really sick and couldn't do what a mom is supposed to do. Now, I know she was depressed, but we didn't talk about that back then. I had to become Daddy's little helper and care for the younger ones. Who else could?

Protective Behavior:

My way of dealing with the feeling of being useless and things falling apart because of me is to keep myself stuck in depression. That way, I never have to risk

the pain of not being helpful to others and feeling like things will fall apart if I
can't do my job of being useful, and it will be my fault.

Your reflection and assessment process focuses on making **a written statement of the threat prediction and a succinct statement of the protective behavior** you use to protect yourself from that threat. That exploration involves tuning into the feelings, emotions, and sensations that you experience when triggered and identifying the threatening learning associated with them.

In Chapter Six, I discussed five primary threats that we experience as young human beings: **abandonment, rejection, physical endangerment, engulfment, and betrayal**. You may encounter feelings and thoughts associated with these experiences. That is not unusual and indicates that you are discovering important information. Remember, what you are experiencing is a memory, although it may feel like it is happening in the present. If the feelings get too intense and threatening, stop the exercise and take a break. You may need to get help from a therapist or someone who can be with you as you explore what may feel like dark and forbidden places.

Think about Joseph Campbell's inspiring words: *"The cave you fear to enter holds the treasure that you seek."*

I have found that the best way to identify threat predictions is to look underneath our activated protective behaviors. (Earlier in this book, I referred to this work as **emotional archaeology**.) What drives those behaviors is a pain-infused emotional learning that has been triggered. To support that process, I have categorized our protective behaviors into three groups:

1. Behavior patterns, both context-specific and non-context-specific;
2. Negative emotional-thought patterns and self-deprecating beliefs and stories;
3. Emotional state patterns linked to depressive symptoms and hypervigilant anxiety.

Behavior Patterns

Context-specific behavior:

Typically, context-specific behavior occurs in specific circumstances or when interacting with particular individuals, for example, at work or with family. In the theater of your mind, imagine doing the behavior that you feel you must not do in that context. As you imagine this, reflect on the following questions and write down what comes.

Notice whatever comes to mind and write it down. Your thinking brain may question what comes up. Notice what it is doing because it probably doesn't understand what you are becoming aware of. Let your emotional brain 'speak' to you when you think about the action you want to do, and what it says will happen to you if you do.

- What do you see or feel others will do when you do what you feel you must not do?
- What are your feelings telling you will happen as a result of doing what you feel you must not do? What do they specifically say will happen to you?
- Does anything about this feeling or threat remind you of past experiences?

Let me give you a brief example of a context-specific problem. Peter wanted to talk with his wife, Josie, about his experience that she seldom listens to him, directs their conversations to herself, and thus rarely asks him about his feelings and thoughts. As a result, he felt unimportant and invisible to her. It had been a problem for him for years, but the thought of talking to her caused him a great deal of anxiety. He knew that he was important to her and that she would never intentionally ignore him, but that didn't change anything except to make him feel selfish for wanting her attention.

To discover what was driving his anxiety, he recalled a recent experience and imagined himself telling her his experience and its aftermath. As he reflected on what he was experiencing, he became aware of this: *"If I tell Josie how I feel, she will feel like it is her fault and that I am criticizing and blaming her. I will hurt her, and it will be my fault, just like it was always my fault when I got into arguments with my younger brother and was isolated in my room as punishment. It is always my fault if something bad happens, and I will get punished."* His protection from this threat was to pretend that his conversations with Josie were okay and suppress his feelings, while he grew increasingly resentful of her behavior and withdrew further. Once he identified this trigger and put words to it, he could move on to update that learning and have a much-needed conversation with Josie. He also recognized that Josie did not intend for him to experience her as ignoring him and cutting him off; it was her protective behavior.

Non-context-specific Behavior:

Non-context-specific behavior occurs in many different circumstances or when interacting with people in general. In the theater of your mind, imagine doing the behavior you feel you must not do in a general context. As you imagine this, reflect on the following questions and write down what comes:

- What do you see or feel that others will do when you do what you feel you must not do?
- What are your feelings telling you will happen if you do what you want to do but feel you must not do? What do they specifically say will happen to you?
- Does anything about this feeling or threat remind you of past experiences? If so, what are they?

For example, the anxious Mr. Nice Guy I discussed in Chapter One manifested in various circumstances. As I explored that part of me, I saw evidence of its emergence in high school. I attended an all-boys Catholic school and learned very quickly how to adapt to that world to avoid conflicts, bullying, and the shame of feeling like I wasn't good enough. Of course, I was unaware of what my emotional brain was learning during this period.

In the context of the threat that you have clarified, think about and reflect on the history of the protective behavior that you have identified. This exercise involves going back as far as you can and examining your life experiences to identify how and when you might have developed the behavior pattern that you use today, the pattern you want to change.

You might find it helpful to review the three Rs of rules, roles, and relating that I discussed in Chapter Three. What can you identify today about the way these three Rs played out in your family? In hindsight, can you see how you may have adapted to them and how that adaptation process still may be playing out today concerning the problem you have identified?

1. Negative emotional-thought patterns, and self-deprecating beliefs and stories. Patterns involving harsh and negative self-talk usually accompany other protective behaviors. However, I have found that identifying the protective nature of these inner dialogues can provide insight into other protective mechanisms. These questions, similar to those used to assess depressive symptoms, can help you identify the protective role they play.

- What would be the positive difference in your life if these emotional-thought patterns did not have their inhibiting influence over you? What would you be doing that these patterns stop you from doing?
- When you imagine experiencing the positive difference you desire and doing what you are prevented from doing, do other problems arise that you were unaware of?
- Is there a history to this way of thinking and feeling about yourself? What factors may have contributed to you acquiring these negative emotional learnings about yourself?

For example, Troy told me about his strong negative emotional-thought pattern: *"I'm just a useless piece of shit that nobody wants to be around."* Initially, specific circumstances that triggered that corrosive thought pattern were difficult for him to identify because, as he stated, "I can't remember not feeling that way about myself."

As he explored what lay underneath that feeling, Troy recognized that the only way he could have a relationship with his narcissistic father was to degrade himself—feeling good about himself and doing well elicited his father's wrath, judgment, and harsh criticism. Although he was no longer in contact with his father, and despite several years of psychotherapy, the emotional residue of the relationship still held him back and was reflected in his threat prediction and protection statement: *"If I do well and feel good about myself, I will still never be good enough for my father's approval and will be rejected by him. The way I deal with this feeling is to tell myself I am a useless piece of shit that nobody wants to be around, and keep to myself so that no one ever sees what I feel about myself. Doing that is safer than risking being rejected as a useless piece of shit".*

Emotional State Patterns

Depressive Symptoms

This assessment is intended for those who experience what I referred to in Chapter Six as an exogenous depression. If you are suffering from depressive symptoms, imagine being <u>symptom-free</u> and then address these questions:

- What are you doing now that these symptoms prohibited you from doing before?
- How are others responding to you being symptom-free?
- What choices can you make that you could not make before, and what is it like to have these choices now?
- Now that you are symptom-free, do other problems arise of which you were unaware?

For example, Johnson's parents were very accomplished professionals in their field of research. When I met him, he was in his early thirties, and despite his graduate education, he reported that he consistently found himself in dead-end jobs. What prompted him to seek help was his struggle with depression. As he looked back on his life, he recognized some feelings that told him that he would never be good enough, no matter how hard he tried, that began to emerge in middle and high school. It wasn't something that he could attribute to his parents, who were always encouraging and supportive of him.

However, he recalled how often their friends and other family members would comment jokingly about the high bar that he had to meet to match his parents' success and what a challenge it would be to ensure that he measured up. They may have intended to motivate him, but what he learned had a paralyzing influence on his life. He was able to identify that being depressed was the way that he kept himself from feeling that he would never meet the challenge and be an embarrassment to his parents. Although no one ever said that to him, that was the knowledge that his emotional brain acquired and what felt true to him when he could put words to the feeling beneath the depressive symptoms.

His threat prediction and protection statement referenced this dilemma: *"If I embarrass my parents by never measuring up to their accomplishments, then they will feel like they have failed as parents, and it will be my fault. They have supported and loved me, and I could not do that to them. I must make sure I never embarrass them by not being as good as them, and I do that by being depressed."*

Generalized Anxiety

If you are experiencing hypervigilant anxiety, I strongly recommend that you undertake this assessment with a psychotherapist. This assessment is intended to be used for problems related to generalized anxiety. We have different phrases we often use to describe hypervigilant anxiety. Some examples include 'walking on eggshells,' 'waiting for the other shoe to drop', or 'something bad is waiting just around the corner.' It is often experienced as a bodily sense of apprehension and cautious awareness.

If you are coping with symptoms of generalized anxiety, imagine being symptom-free and then address these questions:

- What are you doing now that these symptoms prevented you from doing before?
- How are others responding to you being symptom-free?
- What choices can you make that you could not make before, and what is it like to have these choices now?
- Now that you are symptom-free, do other problems arise of which you were unaware?

For example, Janna, a 27-year-old nurse, identified an emotional learning pattern that, when triggered, caused her to become excessively apprehensive and nervous and experience an anxious need always to have everything in order. When she described her behavior, she referred to herself jokingly as having OCD or obsessive-compulsive disorder. After clarifying the threat prediction and her associated anxious cautiousness to ensure everything was in order, she spent about two weeks observing its activation.

This is what she told me in a session after this observation period:

"I carried that statement with me and either looked at it or remembered it whenever I started to feel that anxious feeling. Wow, I didn't realize how often that happens. And it was just so many little things. I started laughing at myself after about a week of using it, and just stopped myself and thought, "Wait a minute! Am I really going to be judged as useless and stupid and be rejected if everything isn't in perfect order? Yes, it is essential to keep things in order on the unit, but I don't need to do that with such anxious compulsiveness. And I also started to feel tenderness for that little girl in me who learned that is what she had to do to avoid being harshly judged and rejected."

After you have written down the threat prediction, the next action is to **clarify how you protect yourself from the painful threat**

your brain predicts will happen. Although you, like many folks, may feel uncomfortable using verbs such as 'must' or 'have to,' please keep this in mind: **If you had a choice about the behavior, then it would not be a problem for you.** But it is **an emotional necessity**. Just as your immune system fights off pathogenic harm, your brain fights off emotional pain and harm.

You may encounter inner resistance to acknowledging that the problem you have been trying to change is a behavior your brain uses to protect you from pain and suffering your brain is predicting you will experience. That resistance is a result of encountering the paradigm shift. It may be challenging to 'own' your behavior if it involves emotional state patterns such as depression or anxiety. Remember, if you had a conscious choice, you most likely would not choose those problems. By doing this work, you will be giving yourself an option to have agency over your life.

You can refer back to the problem statement you wrote in Chapter Eight for clues in clarifying your protective behavior. It can also be beneficial for Step Four in the next chapter to identify any history associated with when this behavior may have started and the context.

Step #3: Observe and Validate

> After you have completed the assessment of your threat prediction and associated protective behavior, I encourage you to spend about a week observing them in your life. This is similar to the observation process in Step One when you were focusing on validating the problem and your desired change.

When I discuss this observation and validation step with my clients, they often ask me why I would want them to think about and affirm experiences that are so negative. That is a reasonable and good question! After all, they want to move forward with the transformation process, particularly after identifying the trigger that drives the problem.

I explain that the underlying principle that informs this five-step transformational process is this: ***By becoming aware of the threat prediction*** *causing the problem you want to eliminate, you can then proceed to Step Four and identify information that corrects that threat prediction. The observation process does not reinforce the learning; it confirms and validates it. It also gives you the opportunity to update it.*

There are two ways to complete this observation and validation process: one is in real-time, and the other is in imaginary emotional time.

Observation in Real-time

There are two reasons that this observation process is beneficial. First, it enables you to **emotionally validate the statement you created** by testing its emotional resonance. Does it feel true to you? Are there better words that capture what you are feeling? Do the feelings and the statement bring up any memories? If so, you will find integrating them into your prediction statement helpful. Remember that the more precise you are about the threat prediction and your protective behavior, the more effective the next phase of transformation will be.

The second advantage of the observation process is that it trains your brain to **practice self-observation and self-awareness without harsh self-judgment**.

Observation in Imagined Time

Observing your prediction and protective behavior statement in real time is not always possible. For example, in the November 2015 workshop, I validated the threat prediction statement and protective behavior I used by recalling memories of wanting to and taking action towards writing. I can assure you that doing so enabled me to verify the threat and the protection I used to withdraw from that threat.

If the problem only appears in certain circumstances, such as when you visit your family or make presentations, I suggest using your memories of these events and recalling your threat prediction to validate it emotionally.

Summary

This chapter explored the second and third steps in a five-step human technology process aimed at achieving enduring personal transformation and becoming trigger-free. It focused on discovering, clarifying, and validating the brain's threat predictions and corresponding protective behaviors.

The Next Vital Step

If the brain predicts a threat, even if it no longer exists, it must protect against it. Thus, as I asked in the Introduction, are we up a creek without a paddle, stuck forever with problem-generating triggers that we can't change? Can we reverse our brain's emotional immunity to change and live a trigger-free life?—Yes. Step Four provides the essential ingredient for that transformation.

As you are now aware of the threat prediction, you can make corrections to it and update the prediction accordingly. After all, that prediction is based upon experiences that happened in the distant past, even though it feels true today.

Chapter Ten
Step Four:

Identify and Clarify Prediction Correction Information and Experiences

Consider how disappointed you feel when expectations aren't met, such as when friends cancel a planned event. Conversely, when negative expectations aren't met—when we expect something unpleasant to happen and instead encounter a positive experience—we often feel relief, surprise, or even joy.

These moments of pleasant surprise are analogous to what the brain experiences when it perceives threat prediction correction information. The most essential aspect for surprising the brain is identifying the information that does not match the brain's predictions. This is the focus of this chapter and Step #4 of our five-step process:

- **Identifying information or creating experiences that contradict and thus correct the threat prediction that you have identified**, so that you can use it to update what your brain has learned.

As many of my clients and I have experienced, you may be surprised that simply becoming aware of the threat prediction often predisposes you to becoming aware of information that leads to a transformative experience. Let's take a more detailed look at the essence of the prediction correction process.

What is the Prediction Correction Process?

The prediction correction process is a neurological mechanism that occurs when the brain recognizes information or experiences that contradict a pain-infused emotional learning. When this happens, the brain unwires the neural network in which the emotional learning is encoded and, in this unwired state, it updates and corrects the old learning with the prediction correction information.

Neuroscience research has demonstrated that the outcome of this unwiring and updating process is an enduring neurological change. Let me share the highlights of a simple personal example to illustrate this point.

I enjoy being an assistant chef for my wife, Patti, who is a culinary wizard. My role involves cleaning up, keeping the prep space clear, chopping and mixing as directed, and lending a hand as best I can.

When Patti corrected my cooking mistakes, I'd feel inadequate and withdraw into silence or use sarcasm to protect myself. After learning about emotional learning and prediction corrections, I realized my triggered feeling stemmed from a threat of rejection. Yet logically, I knew Patti's feedback was about precision, not rejection. Recognizing this mismatch, I replaced the old prediction—*If I make a mistake helping Patti in the kitchen, she will be disappointed in me, and she will reject me*—with the truth: *Mistakes are normal and come with learning. Patti's corrections reflect her precision, not any disappointment in or rejection of me.*

That happened in mid-2018. Today, I laugh and call it out if that old threat gets mildly triggered, knowing that I am becoming more and more trigger-free every time I correct it.

The input required to launch the prediction correction experience is information and experiences that contradict the threat the brain predicts will happen when an emotional learning is triggered. I refer to that input as a *prediction correction statement.*

The Essence of a Prediction Correction Statement

A prediction correction statement is a written description of information and/ or experiences that contradict what the brain predicts will happen in a specific context. That context can be an event, an interaction, a situation, or a person.

For example, if the brain predicts shame and rejection in a particular situation based on what it has learned, then the prediction correction will contradict that prediction in that context. In this case, the mismatch experience may be appreciation and acknowledgement. The brain recognizes the mismatch and unwires the emotional learning neural network that generated the threat prediction and then updates it.

This update process can be intentionally set up, and Chapter Eleven discusses four methods for doing so.

After nine years of helping people and myself learn to live a trigger-free life, I have identified six factors that can make identifying prediction corrections and experiences challenging. I share them here so that you are aware of them in your process.

The Challenges of Identifying Prediction Correction Information

Let me introduce the first challenge with a question:

When was the last time that you reflected on your life for the specific purpose of recalling experiences that contradicted the threat of what you expected and felt would happen at any given moment?

Yes, we can recall explicit positive experiences associated with specific people, events, or interactions; however, we don't do that to identify prediction corrections that we can use to update old emotional learnings. The point is that for most of us, this process requires **a very different way of thinking about change and transformation.**

Second, prediction corrections are **not affirmations or positive thinking**. These have a place in reinforcing the positive beliefs and stories we create, which we can associate with pleasant experiences. However, they also tend to be generalizations that lack sufficiently specific contextual information to be associated with a threat prediction. That does not mean that they are not valuable. In this respect, I would like to share with you an approach to strengthen positive experiences highlighted below.

Frequently, I ask my clients and workshop participants this question: When you have a positive experience, like being recognized for or feeling good about your work performance, achieving a workout goal, enjoying time with family or friends, or just having a great day, what do you do with that experience? The most common answer is nothing.

Ahhh! However, if just one negative or upsetting thing happens, the brain can have a field day, and it's not fun. I suggest an alternative to doing nothing when you have positive experiences, which I briefly discussed in the section entitled 'Are There Positive Triggers?' in Chapter Nine. I call it the SFT process.

SFT is an acronym for SEE-FEEL-THINK. Although it is not an essential element of this book, I believe it is a beneficial process to be aware of and practice. The basic premise of the SFT process is this: by intentionally focusing on the positive experiences you have throughout your day, you create memories that can become prediction corrections that you can use as you follow the path of living a trigger-free life. (Details in the Appendix, Section #2.)

Third, your prediction correction must **closely match the contents of the prediction threat**. I suggest that you consider the five major threats I identified in Chapter Six: abandonment, rejection, betrayal, physical endangerment, and engulfment. For example, if you identify rejection or abandonment associated with the threat you have predicted, then the correction statement will include information and experiences that contradict that prediction.

Fourth, the prediction correction information may involve acknowledging that **the people associated with the threat are no longer alive or unable to inflict harm**. It may seem strange to say that your thinking brain knows they have passed on or are not present in your life, but your emotional brain doesn't. Threats associated with them may 'haunt' you because the learning you acquired in the relationship still exists in your emotional brain.

For example, Suzanne knew her elderly, feeble father could no longer threaten her with abandonment, but her emotional learning about what she learned in her relationship with him still resonated as an emotional truth. Or think about Cyrus, one of the examples in Chapter Nine, who had to stay busy because the threat of physical endangerment associated with his father felt true in the present, even though his father had passed away nearly 15 years before he became aware of that pain-infused learning.

When you pair the threat prediction with the prediction correction information, the brain updates itself and corrects that time distortion. Then the past truly becomes the past!

Fifth, as you search for corrective information, you may find yourself **slipping into counteractive thinking mode**. Like the counteractive approaches that I discussed in the Introduction, counteractive thinking seeks to override or overcome what feels real to you but is also irrational and makes no sense. When that happens, you are experiencing the conflict between your rational, logical thinking brain's assessment of your emotional brain's learning and the associated threat prediction, as I described in Chapter Five. Judging that a threat prediction is irrational may describe the threat accurately, but that judgment is not the contradiction that disproves the threat or changes the fact that the threat, when activated, feels real to the survival-biased brain.

Sixth, the prediction correction may involve **observations of others who seemed to be able to do what you want to do**. For example, one of Suzanne's observations was that her friends and coworkers were able to express themselves without being rejected or judged, as she had feared would happen if she followed their example. She had noticed this on many occasions, but that observation alone was not enough to update her brain. That observation needs to be paired with the threat prediction in an activated state, as you will learn in Chapter Eleven.

For quick reference, here is a bullet-point summary of the challenges:

- This is a different way of thinking about change.
- Prediction corrections aren't affirmations.
- Prediction corrections must closely match the threat's specifics.
- Historical context may show the threat never existed.
- Be aware of the tendency to use counteractive thinking.
- Observing others successfully managing similar issues can help.

With these considerations in mind, let's look at some approaches that you can take to identify information and experiences that contradict and thus have the potential to correct the threat prediction that you clarified.

Identifying and Clarifying Prediction Corrections

There are two basic prediction correction categories:

1. Knowledge from your life experiences and
2. Correction experiences you create with new experiences.

Knowledge from Your Life Experiences

This approach involves scanning your life for evidence that contradicts your identified threat. In effect, you are looking for:

1. Interactions and situations when you acted on the desired change and suffered none of the threatening outcomes that your statement predicted, or

2. Historical information that shows you that the threat never really existed in the first place.

My 2015 workshop experience of eliminating my writing procrastination is a good example of scanning for contrary evidence. I paired my threat prediction of being shamed and rejected if I wrote another book with many experiences of feeling competent and being complimented and appreciated for my work and what I had written. You will read other examples of how individuals found evidence that contradicted the threat prediction in this chapter.

Let me provide a brief example of identifying historical information that demonstrates the threat never really existed in the first place. The fact that a threat never really existed does not mean the emotional brain did not learn something that it experienced as a threat.

Jake is a 34-year-old HR manager. He contacted me to break a self-sabotaging relationship cycle: *"When it feels like the other shoe is going to drop, I panic and try harder, and that never works. I push my partners away with my anxiety."* He identified the threat and protective behavior: *"If I experience unpredictability in my intimate relationships, it means that something bad is going to happen to me, and there is nothing I can do about it. I will be all alone and powerless to do anything about what is going to happen to me. To protect myself from this feeling, I became anxious and needy for predictability, and cling to my partner as if my life depended on her."*

He had done a few years of psychotherapy in his mid-twenties. The focus was on understanding and managing his anxiety and the influence of many uprooting experiences during his childhood. His father died when he was three years old, and his mother moved about every nine months or so to find work until she remarried when he was fourteen. Jake had developed some practical ways to manage his relationship anxiety and would also try to explain it to his partners, hoping that they would understand. Still, that didn't change his feeling that the slightest bit of unpredictability threatened his world. For example, when a partner did not return his text messages within a short period, the threat was activated, and the anxious clinging followed.

When Jake scanned his history for experiences that contradicted the threat, he found warm memories of his uncle, Tony. During the many moves, he recalled how Uncle Tony always helped and told Jake that he was always just a phone call away. He always made sure that Jake and his mother were settled in and would call him frequently. As Jake recalled these memories, he realized that Uncle Tony had ensured that all was well and that nothing bad had ever happened. Yes, his threat prediction felt true, but he had never paired it with the truth of his lived experience: *"While unpredictability can be uncomfortable for me, there are caring people and friends who can provide support and understanding, just as my Uncle Tony did. I am not powerless when things are unpredictable, and I can remember my Uncle Tony's love and care. Even if the other shoe drops, I know I will be okay because I always have been."*

After they complete their discovery work, I have seen many instances when clients report feeling an internal shift during the observation process discussed in Chapter Nine. It seems that simply being aware of and observing the threat and the protective behavior can often provide the ingredients for them to recognize prediction corrections and thus create a transformative emotional experience.

We have discussed finding prediction correction experiences by exploring the past. Now, let's discuss creating them in new experiences.

Prediction Corrections that You Create from New Experiences

As I just mentioned, it can happen that simply being aware of the threat prediction and its associated protective behavior provides the 'grist for the mill' for an update to occur with new experiences. Clients have frequently described how their awareness of the threat being triggered in the present brings their focus to what is happening within them and around them, and presents opportunities to create contradictory experiences in the present. Sometimes, these opportunities involve a conscious pairing process that updates the threat. Let me tell you a story about Jackson's experience of a negative expectation (a threat) meeting a positive experience.

When a Negative Expectation Meets a Positive Experience

Jackson was invited to a college friend's wedding and looked forward to seeing classmates he hadn't talked with for almost seven years. He also knew that Carol, his college girlfriend, would be there and felt uneasy about seeing her. The breakup she initiated was abrupt and hard on him, and the sting of that experience still lingered whenever he thought about her. Questions cascaded through his mind for several weeks before the event and were the focus of a few sessions: "*What will I say? What will she say? Will she ignore me? Should I ignore her? Will she be with someone?*" Just the thought of seeing her triggered him. In addition, he told me that most of the people there knew their history and that this generated more questions that swirled in his mind: "*How will they feel, and what will they say and do? Will everyone pretend it never happened? Is that what I should do?*"

Jackson was expecting an uncomfortable experience (a prediction), given the painful feelings that he felt when he thought of Carol and the breakup. The fact that she would be there wouldn't stop him from going, but just the thought of seeing her generated a feeling that he wanted to avoid. He also recognized the feelings as familiar from other relationship endings and wanted to understand more about what was happening within him.

He and I had been working on one specific triggering experience that was the source of a great deal of anxiety for him, and it was showing up in anticipation of the wedding and seeing Carol. It concerned the threat of being rejected and humiliated after a relationship ends, a learning he attributed to a traumatic high school experience. He had a close and secret relationship with Robin, a classmate during his eleventh and twelfth grades. They had to keep it a secret because her parents were adamantly opposed to it. On the night of high school graduation, she told her parents she was going to a party with her girlfriends. Her parents followed her, and they intervened when they saw her with Jackson. He described his experience this way: "*Her dad was so angry; I thought he was going to hit me. His red face and eyes were bulging, and he shouted right into my face, "I don't ever want to see you with my daughter again! You jackass! You're not good enough for her and never will be."* He recalled how the other kids walked away quickly as Robin's father grabbed her arm and yelled, *"Don't ever lie to me again."*

Jackson had done EMDR to ameliorate some of the trauma of that scene, and he reported that he felt much less anxious and distressed when bringing the memory up. But the thought of seeing Carol at the wedding was causing him great distress. It was triggering him. He wrote a statement about the threat prediction associated with Carol and discussed his plan to monitor his emotions and assess the validity of the prediction during the wedding. *He said, "At least I will know what's going on instead of being stuck in anxiety and feeling powerless. Just having that awareness brings some relief and sense of control."*

Jackson noticed her walk in as folks gathered for a pre-wedding day get-together. The discomfort came on full throttle. He wondered if he should approach her or wait for her to approach him. She greeted him and asked if he'd be open to talking later. Despite his anxiety and discomfort, he agreed to meet after dinner.

When they met, she apologized for the abrupt way that she had ended the relationship and explained what had been happening in her life that had led to the breakup. Jackson felt her sincerity and sadness about the breakup. As their conversation concluded, Jackson noticed that his experience of her and the conversation were contrary to his threat of being rejected by her. After the wedding, they wished each other all the best with a warm hug.

On the way home, Jackson thought about her and their conversation. The sting of the breakup was barely noticeable, replaced by a touch of sadness and a sense of completion. His expectation of distress and awkward discomfort was met with a different experience. The breakup wasn't about him not being good enough, as he felt and thought; it was about some challenges in her family and her feeling responsible for helping them. This information and her affirmation of him contradicted his "I'm not good enough for her" feeling. When he shared that with her during their conversation, she responded with a hug and heartfelt reassurance that this was never the case, affirming what a loving and good person he was in her eyes and how glad she was that he had been part of her life.

What happened to the memory of that stinging breakup experience? The scene of it didn't disappear—he could still recall the place and evening when it happened—but the emotional hurt was hardly a whisper. The experience was now just a memory from his past, not a painful experience that the thought of her triggered in the present.

Simply put, Jackson was aware of what he was feeling and thinking when they began talking, as well as how he felt during his interaction with Carol. They were completely different. He created a mismatch between what he expected or his brain predicted would happen and what did happen, and he both felt and shared that mismatch with Carol. His recognition, and, thus, his brain's recognition of this mismatch, caused his brain to unwire the memory and the learning of the hurtful sting of the breakup. That unwiring process enabled the learning update to happen.

The key to this unwiring and updating process was Jackson's conscious and simultaneous recognition of the difference between his feelings and thoughts (the sting and the anxious *"I'm not good enough for her."*) and what she communicated. He used this experience as a prediction correction. Trigger be gone!

You Might Be Surprised Too!

Jackson was aware of the threat he was experiencing before the wedding weekend, but he had not identified any contradictory information. However, he recognized that the threat and his experience of Carol contradicted each other. He used that information to not only update his brain in real-time but also to write a prediction correction statement that he used to reinforce the new learning using the Two-hand Process, which I will discuss in Chapter Eleven.

This was also how Jill, from Chapter Seven, transformed her social anxiety. Her threat prediction and protection statement read as follows: *If people see me as the needy person I feel I am, they will judge me as being immature, like a needy child who is a burden to her mother. They will ignore me, and I will be alone with just myself. I must never be seen as needy by anyone. To deal with the threat of this feeling, I become anxious and quiet, and withdraw like a wallflower. That way, no one will see me as the needy person I feel I am, and they won't judge and reject me.*

Recall that she went to some holiday parties and, with her statement in hand, observed her experience as she interacted with folks. Having the statement in hand enabled her to understand what was happening and its origins in her childhood, not in the present moment. She interacted with and engaged with people, discovering that the threat had no basis in her current reality. She felt the anxiety and still engaged with people anyway, a pairing process I will discuss in Chapter Eleven.

The contradictory statement that she wrote later stated: *Even though I learned to be afraid that people would see me as immature, like a needy child who places demands on her mother, my experiences tell me I am a positive, curious, and open adult. No one has ever rejected me for being that way—just the opposite—I like people, and people like me.* Like Jackson, she used the Two-hand Process to reinforce the update process afterward.

You may also have experiences similar to Jackson, Jill, and many other clients: **Simply knowing what your triggered experience is all about (your written threat prediction statement) when you feel triggered can often become the catalyst to help you recognize contradictory information and introduce it to your brain simultaneously.**

One of the most common examples of this involves compliments. If you're like many people, you become uncomfortable when you receive a compliment. You may minimize the compliment or distract the person complimenting you with a self-deprecating joke (that was my favorite protective mechanism when I was complimented). If this resonates with you, consider it an opportunity to become trigger-free when you are complimented.

First, identify the threat and protection associated with being given a compliment. For me, it was this: when people compliment me, they will eventually see that I am not really what they think I am, and will withdraw and talk about me as a fake. I dealt with this feeling by telling them jokingly, *"Yeah, I have everybody fooled,"* or replying with a quick and insincere thank you. When I understood and recognized what was happening, I started accepting compliments and relishing being seen for my competence. My reply now is, *"Thank you. I enjoy what I do and always seek ways to improve."* So far, no one has ever withdrawn from me or accused me of being a fake, and if they did, I hope I'd have an opportunity to inquire about their experience.

Nine Examples of Prediction Correction Statements

The following prediction corrections are related to the nine examples I presented in Chapters Eight and Nine. To respect your reading time, I will only present the desired change, the threat prediction, and the associated prediction correction for each example. Please note that, in some instances, these prediction corrections have been paired with their associated threats as an outcome of the client's experience of becoming aware of this information:

1. **Pauline**

   Desired Change: *I want to stay calm and curious with my friends and people at work when they are talking about their different experiences.*

   Threat Prediction: *If people are talking about their activities and what they are doing as a family, I will be ignored and become invisible, just like what happened in Middle School when all the kids talked about their vacations and what their families were doing. I felt so left out that I just withdrew because I felt like I wasn't good enough. That all changed in high school because my mom started working. We had more money and did more things. That's when I started to feel like I had to jump in so my classmates would know I was just as good as them, just like I must do with my friends today. If I don't, I will feel the same awful feelings I felt back then.*

   Prediction Correction: *I know this feels true today, and the feeling of being left out and excluded felt true in middle school. But that was middle school and is old history. I remember many times over the past several years when I felt that anxiety and didn't jump in. I just let myself chill and listen to all the chatter. Folks often asked me what was happening in my life and how the kids were doing. I also know I can engage people without having to play the one-up game. I feel sad about what happened during middle school. If I could go back in time, I'd tell my younger self that we'll get through this rough patch and come out okay.*

2. **Simone**

Desired Change:

I have imagined myself talking with Jeremy about how depressed and tired I feel, and that I need him to step up and even recommend counseling for us. I want to make that image a reality and have the conversation I keep avoiding. It is the conversation I know my mother never had with my dad, and it took a big toll on her.

Threat Prediction:

If I do what my mother never did, I will cause great harm to Jeremy, and it will be my fault. But if I don't, I will continue down the road of depression and resentment. I don't know how I can do this when the kids go to college; they keep me distracted and busy. But after they leave, my life will be empty, just like my mother's. But if I talk with him and he falls apart, then I am stuck with him, which feels unbearable. Then, I would need to get a divorce, and my mother would feel like she wasted her life, and it would be my fault she felt that way. That would make me a very selfish person who doesn't deserve love.

Prediction Correction:

The biggest threat to me is that my kids hate me for hurting him. But will they really hate me? That is way too big for me to answer. What I do know is that I hate myself and feel like I am breaking down. I know I will survive the stress of talking with Jeremy when I tell him about my concerns for him, me, and our marriage. All these years, I have never said a word. I just had to be the quiet, good wife who supports her husband, just like my suffering mother. I would never have hated my mother if she had left my dad. As hard as she tried to pretend, I knew she was miserable. It would not have been easy, but looking back now, I wish she had done that. Even if the kids hate me, at least they will have a mother who isn't depressed, having to pretend she is okay. I know I can work it out with them.

3. **Gary**

   Desired Change:

   I want to trust that I can be in a stable, close relationship in which I feel I can be open and caring without feeling like I am never doing anything right because I never know what right is, because it is constantly changing.

   Threat Prediction:

   If I get too close to someone and start to care for them and let them care for me, the other shoe will always drop, and they will switch on me and reject me. It will be just like it was at home with my mother. I was either her favorite, or she ignored me like I didn't matter. I never knew which mother would show up. I know how to survive ups and downs, but stability is unpredictable and actually scary.

   Prediction Correction:

   My mother had a serious mental problem, which my father and her family ignored. When I look at my relationships, I see how I need to create chaos for myself because I learned how to survive chaos. Knowing that stability is threatening feels strangely true, and it is also freeing. I recall two significant relationships that felt easy and open and went well until I started to get anxious, and now I know why. I have developed many friendships that feel stable and supportive to me. And even when things get a little rocky because of miscommunication, they have never rejected me.

4. **Nancy**

   Desired Change:

   It is important to me that I stop pretending when I am with my family. I need to tell my mother that I see the world differently from her and that it is okay for me to be that way. I want to let her know I love her and that it makes me sad for her that she sees the world as she does. I also want to let her know that I understand why she does.

   Threat Prediction:

   To belong to the family, everyone must go along with mom and not upset her by disagreeing with her. If I speak up for myself and tell her that I see the world differently, I won't belong anymore and will be left out of family events, even though I don't want to go to most of them anyway. I'd rather go along with everyone than risk not belonging to the family.

Prediction Correction:

I know Mom had a tough childhood and moved in with her sister's family when she was five. From what little she has talked about, the rules were strict, and the punishment harsh. It was a big Catholic family with nine kids. Now that I know about emotional learning, I imagine she learned things about surviving that I can't imagine. No wonder she sees the world the way she sees it. But I don't have to take her sadness and pessimism home after visiting. I don't want to hurt mom, but I can tell her I see the world differently and still love her. If my family is upset with that, I can ask her if it is okay for me to see the world differently from her. I know she will say yes, and even if she doesn't, I can still affirm that I love her. My family isn't going to turn their backs on me because I see the world differently from them, and if they do, I have the communication skills to deal with it. After all, it is my story that they will do that, and I have no basis to believe it except that I've come to feel that way.

5. **Leo**

Desired Change:

I want to be free of the anxiety and threat of being banished if I make a mistake. If I make a mistake, I want to know that I can deal with it.

Threat Prediction:

If I am found guilty of doing something wrong, I will be punished by being ignored and sent into exile, where I will be all alone. I must not be found guilty of doing something wrong, so I must always do things perfectly or find a way to please people so they won't find me guilty.

Prediction Correction:

When I look back, I can see where this comes from. We all had to act like the perfect family. From our clothes to our grades, from church services every Sunday to how we ate our food, there was no room for error. And when we did slip up, we'd always get the look, especially from dad. I thought I had left all that behind when I moved away. But when I remember the look today, I can feel myself being judged and found guilty. But nothing ever happened. I was never exiled or even sent to my room. I know I can handle not being perfect now that I'm in my thirties. It was different for that little guy back then. How could he have known that not being perfect is normal and human? Yeah, I'm not perfect, and I'm not guilty for not being perfect, and I'm not alone. I'm okay, just like that little guy I was back then was okay.

6. **Manny**
   Desired Change:
   The only change I want is to be able to talk with them about how I feel and discuss my concerns about how they feel. I know they know how their mom felt trapped by her mother, and I don't want them to feel the same way.
   Threat Prediction:
   If I talk about what I want in my relationships with Jackson and Jacqui, I feel they will feel I need them to take care of me. I will then be a burden like my mother-in-law, Mary, was for many years to my wife, Sue. They will then be angry at me for being so dependent on them, as Sue felt towards her mother. I will not let them be angry with me for trapping them like Sue was by her mother.
   Prediction Correction:
   I'm not my mother-in-law. I am very independent and have a great circle of friends that I enjoy being with. Sue never had that because Mary sucked all her time and energy. I can talk with Jackson and Jacqui and share my concerns and observations. They are not going to be angry with me for wanting to spend more time with them and their families, and I know they will discuss it. I just never realized that what was causing me so much concern was my feeling that I would be like my mother-in-law was to Sue, a burden that drained the life out of her.

7. **William**
   Desired Change:
   The only change I want is to be able to tell people what I can and can't do when they ask. I want to negotiate different responsibilities with my boss and also set some limits with my wife.

<u>Threat Prediction:</u>

If I don't do what important people in my life ask me to do, they will blame me for their unhappiness, and it will be my fault that their lives will be ruined. I know this sounds ridiculous, and I know it's not true, but it feels so true. I must do what I am asked to do, or else I will suffer the pain of disappointing my family, my parents, and my boss. I will be an irresponsible, undependable person, just like my grandfather. I will be rejected and ignored. People will cut me out of their lives and never let me back in.

<u>Prediction Correction:</u>

I am proud that I am a dependable and responsible person whom others can rely on. My wife isn't going to cut me out of her life if I explain all this to her. She might even be happy to hear that I am finally acknowledging that I also have needs instead of constantly frantically worrying about others and pleasing them. I know my boss knows and values my abilities, and we will be able to explore ways for me to better manage the demands of my position.

8. **Cyrus**

<u>Desired Change:</u>

I want to slow down and hire a manager-type person who can do the running around I have to do. The business can afford it, and I can handle the books, but the daily grind is getting to me. That's hard to admit because I have always worked a lot.

<u>Threat Prediction:</u>

If I free myself from my daily grind and take time for myself, I will be harshly punished, just like my father did if I wasn't always busy doing something. I know he's gone, but the feeling that I will be beaten is still there. I just didn't know how strong it was. He would scream that an idle mind is the devil's workshop as he whipped me with his belt. I must make sure I don't get whipped again.

<u>Prediction Correction:</u>

My father is dead now, and he can't hurt me anymore. I know that. But I didn't realize that his words and his beatings were still affecting me so much. Now I know that I have worked hard so that I wouldn't be punished.

It feels strange to know that, but it makes sense. I built a good life for my family. I can slow down and relax, maybe even take a long vacation with my wife. The past is over, and I am free to chill as my son tells me.

9. **Sally**

Desired Change:

I want to be clear, direct, and respectful in my relationships with my team members. I also want to follow up with them on my requests calmly.

Threat Prediction:

If I am clear, direct, and even respectful in my communication with my team members, they will see me as a bully who doesn't care about their feelings. Then they will leave me, and my practice will fail, and I will fail. As I think about this threat, I can feel it. But I also see where I learned this. The rule in my family was to never ask for what you want because anybody who did was criticized for acting like they were more important than anybody else and accused of being a demanding brat who didn't care for others.

Prediction Correction:

This is my practice, and I am a thoughtful, conscientious dentist who has the best interests of my patients and team in mind. But I have been ignoring my best interests for fear of breaking family rules and being labeled a bully. I find it interesting that many team members keep asking me for more direction, and I have been ignoring their requests. And when I have provided that, they have always acknowledged it. I will meet with them individually and take responsibility for being indirect in my communication. I will tell them I know it has been challenging for them to know what I want because I haven't communicated it clearly. I will also ask them to tell me if they feel I am acting like a bully so that we can discuss it. I don't want to recreate my family rule in my practice.

Suzanne Identifies the Prediction Correction

The last time we checked in with Suzanne, she had discovered the threat prediction that was causing her protective behaviors. The focus of her desired change was to be able to express herself, her thoughts, and her preferences.

After bringing the threat prediction into her conscious awareness, Suzanne identified several experiences in which she had expressed herself and her preferences without being shamed, rejected, or left alone. She also recalled times when her contributions to her work team were acknowledged and appreciated. She also remembered asking her friends to help with a project and expressing her preferences for an activity or plan involving them, and everything went smoothly. Those experiences became prediction corrections that she used to unwire the neural network of the original memory and learning. Because these experiences contradicted the original learning, they became the catalysts for transformation.

She identified the prediction correction: "*Yeah, I learned that if I express myself and ask for what I want, people will shame and reject me, and I will then be all alone. I learned that long ago with my father when I didn't know what I was learning. The truth is that I have many experiences and memories of expressing myself and my opinions, and nothing bad has ever happened. I am creative and love to engage with people.*"

Clarifying Your Prediction Correction

Earlier in this chapter, I suggested two approaches to identifying experiences and information that contradict and thus correct your targeted emotional learning. One involves scanning your life experiences, looking for:

1. Interactions and situations when you acted on the desired change and suffered none of the painful outcomes that your threat statement predicted, and

2. Historical information that shows you the threat may have never really existed in the first place.

The second approach involves engaging in experiences where you feel the now-conscious threat prediction and protective behavior are activated, and then acting in accordance with your desired change while observing the outcome. This is what Jill did. In this case, you are creating a real-time prediction correction and simultaneously pairing it with the threat prediction. When that happens, I suggest writing out a prediction statement to reinforce the transformation. I will discuss this in Chapter Eleven.

There is a third way to clarify a prediction correction, and it is similar to the second way that I just discussed. It is a 'spontaneous transformation' and I will discuss it more in Chapter Eleven. This occurs when you become aware of the threat prediction and realize immediately that it is entirely false based on your life experiences. When that happens, I again suggest writing out the knowledge that makes your threat prediction false so that you can continue the update using one of the protocols I discuss in Chapter Eleven.

To identify past experiences that can serve as prediction corrections, I recommend the following approach:

- Get comfortable in a quiet place. (NOTE: Having your cell phone on record is beneficial so that you can record what comes up without writing it down, which you can do at the end of the process.)
- Read the statements that you have created about the change that you want, the threat associated with that change, and the protective behavior that follows when the threat is activated. Let yourself feel whatever comes to mind.
- Direct your focus to the experience of the threat prediction
- Let yourself journey back in time, looking for instances when experiences and interactions diverged from the threat prediction. Particularly notice when you performed the change that you want, and the threat did not materialize.
- Pay attention to any images or memories that attract your attention and explore them in as much detail as possible.

- Be aware of the tendency to minimize corrective experiences because they are not emotionally intense or feel fleeting in time.
- Listen to the recording of what you observed. Clarify it in writing and set it aside for a few days as you reflect on it.
- Review what you wrote and observe what else comes up. Does what you wrote contradict what the threat predicts? The prediction correction does not have to be precise; it just needs to be related to the threat.
- Keep in mind that you have not paired your prediction correction with the threat, and thus, your nervous system may feel resistant to the correction information. You are reviewing the information with your thinking brain and are not in the felt experience of pairing the threat and the corrective information required for an update to take place.

Summary

This chapter provided a guide for identifying and clarifying threat prediction corrections to update emotional learnings associated with these threat predictions. It is the fourth step of a five-step process aimed at helping you transform your emotional reactions and live a trigger-free life by consciously pairing threat predictions with contradictory experiences.

Dear Brain, You Need an Update, and I Have Some New Information to Help You with That

We have now reached the step that makes this 5-step human technology truly transformative. Now you have the opportunity to introduce your brain to the information that will enable it to update itself, allowing it to better support you in experiencing the life, love, and success you desire.

Chapter Eleven presents Step Five and four different ways to pair the threat prediction with the prediction correction to launch the prediction correction and update process.

Chapter Eleven

Make Your Brain Right by Making It Wrong:

A 5-step Human Technology for Enduring Transformation

Have you thought about making something that you learned wrong when you know it is right?

The obvious answer is no—even the question itself can stir up some frustration or confusion. What possible reason would anyone have to do that?

However, that is what this book recommends concerning pain-infused emotional learnings that *feel* right.

At this point, I am confident that you are aware that we all have acquired knowledge about interacting in the world that we didn't know we acquired. Some of that knowledge, when activated, sparks experiences of positive energy—we know these as feelings such as love, joy, delight, happiness, calmness, connection, curiosity, belonging, and caring. However, some of that knowledge, when activated, triggers experiences of pain and suffering associated with unsafeness, danger, loss, and even terror.

Pain-infused emotional learning, acquired without awareness, becomes our triggers. Much of it is wrong and no longer applies in our adult life, but it feels right! We need to update that knowledge and, in essence, correct it!

Before I introduce the fifth step of the five-step process of becoming trigger-free, I want to summarize the first four:

1. Clarify the problem and your desired change concerning it.
2. Discover and validate the threat prediction and your protective behavior.

3. Observe and test the emotional resonance of the threat prediction.
4. Identify prediction correction experiences.

This chapter introduces and illustrates:

- The **prediction correction process**.
- Spontaneous transformation and **Trigger-informed Mindfulness**.
- **Four ways to make your brain right by making it wrong.**
- Nine examples of the prediction correction process.

The Prediction Correction Process

The purpose of the prediction correction process is to update the threat-infused emotional learning that your emotional brain, unbeknownst to you, acquired in the past. That update process is the outcome of pairing the now explicit threat prediction with information that contradicts it. Illustration 11.1 portrays the three essential activities of the pairing process that launch this update process.

1. Activate the threat prediction so it is a felt experience in the present, and bring your statement of it into your field of awareness.
2. When the threat prediction is activated, bring the prediction correction information into your conscious awareness.
3. Focus on the difference between the threat prediction and the prediction correction information using one of the four techniques discussed in this chapter.

Illustration 11.1 – The Prediction Correction Process

The numbers in the illustration correspond with the explanations below.

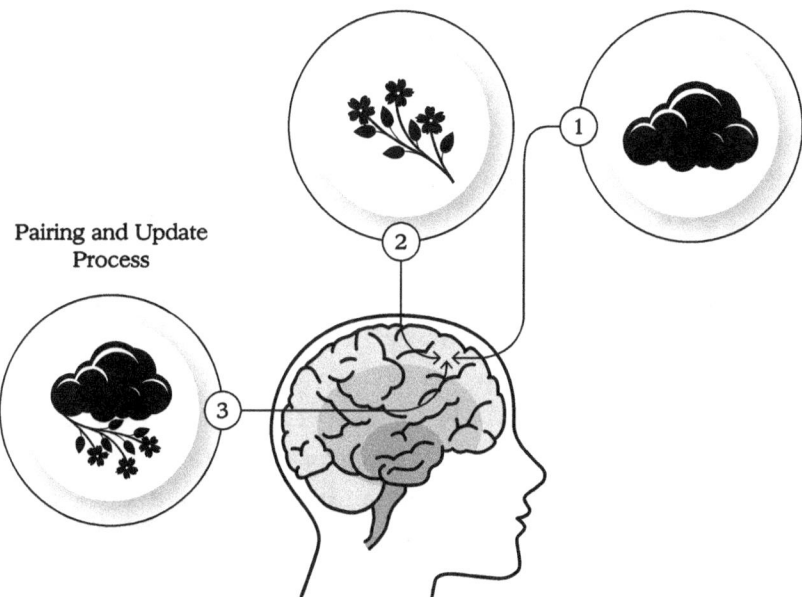

Threat Prediction Correction
- But what about...
- However...
- Wait a minute...
- That's not what I know to be true...
- My experience tells me this...

Threat prediction
If this... then this...

Pairing and Update Process

The application of the correction protocol assumes that you have a written statement of:

- The Threat Prediction and Protective Behavior you clarified in Chapter Nine (suggested format: *If I do this ... then this will happen (your description of the pain and suffering you will experience). To protect myself from this experience with this feeling, I must ... (your description of your protective behavior)*
- The Threat Prediction Correction Information you identified in Chapter Ten.

This pairing process is akin to being in an art museum and intentionally comparing two pictures within your field of vision. As I discussed in Chapter Seven, this purposely directed process optimizes your survival-biased brain's natural learning, predicting, and adapting process. The brain has to update itself in the best interest of your survival!

We are partnering with evolution to create the new, rather than fighting it to change the old.

This approach differs significantly from the numerous counteractive interventions designed to replace negative, pain-infused memories and learnings with new, positive ones. Using the counteractive approach, the original negative memory and learning remain in place and are not altered. The new positive memory or thought is thus competing with the old negative one for your attention when the old one is activated. It is a change that produces no real change, and guess which memory often wins out.

21st-century neuroscience research has also identified that **this unwired neural network remains in its open and receptive state for approximately 5 hours.** After that 5-hour window, it rewires (reconsolidates) itself and locks in the updated information. During the 5-hour window, you can **continue to strengthen the new by updating the old with the correction information**. In essence, you do this by continuing the pairing process. Trigger, be updated! Trigger, be gone!

This chapter discusses four ways that you can update a pain-infused emotional learning. However, before I delve into that topic, I would like to briefly discuss an experience that many of my clients have had in sessions as well as in their daily lives when they are aware of these emotional learnings. It is a topic I briefly discussed in the previous chapter when referring to 'spontaneous transformation.' There is an awareness technique that I call 'Trigger-informed Mindfulness' that can predispose us to spontaneous transformation.

Spontaneous Transformation and Trigger-informed Mindfulness

I believe that 'spontaneous transformation' occurs quite frequently throughout our lives. We are just not aware of it. For example, have you had a discussion with family members about a past event that has a negative association for you, and are surprised to hear that others had a completely different experience from yours? If you are open to their experience, you may feel a shift within you as you rethink and reimagine your memory of that event. (Please note that I am not referring to a family's denial of abuse.)

Chapter One discussed common examples of how learning updates related to skills and knowledge happen in everyday lives. These can occur spontaneously and unintentionally or intentionally. We are also familiar with the steps that we can take to intentionally update information that we recognize contains errors or needs an update. However, we can experience spontaneous updates of information that we are not consciously aware of learning.

For example, let's say that you are at a party, and your friend Gavin introduces you to one of his friends, Randy, whom you have never met. After conversing for a few minutes, you feel a dislike for Randy. You're not sure why, but you withdraw from the conversation and avoid him for the rest of the evening. All you know is that something about Randy's energy or attitude bothered you. Several weeks later, your friends are gathering again for a card party. Randy is there again and walks over to you. Instantly, you feel the uncomfortable vibe associated with him. He smiles at you and begins a conversation, *"Hey, we didn't get a chance to get acquainted at the last party, and I'd like to get to know you. I was not very friendly to anyone that weekend. I had to put my dog, Stoopie, to sleep on the day of the party. I probably shouldn't have shown up, but Gavin thought it would help me get out of my funk, so I said yes. You know how he is always taking care of folks."*

You feel a shift as you both talk about everything from his dog's passing to your mutual interests in hiking, from the kind of Bourbon you both like to the challenges of your careers. The evening ends, and now you feel a warmth towards and curiosity about him. The feeling of dislike and need to withdraw are gone; instead, you find that you are interested in hanging out and getting to know him better. How did that shift take place?

Your brain had learned to associate an uncomfortable feeling with Randy, and, quite naturally, it caused you to withdraw and avoid him. You were aware of this and felt the same feelings as he walked up to you during your second get-together. However, your experience was very different. What your brain predicted based upon what it had learned (and thus what you were feeling) and what you experienced were very different. By being aware of the difference between what you originally learned about Randy and what you experienced at the second gathering, you enabled your brain to update itself with the new experience because it contradicted what it had learned about him previously.

We all have experiences like this, and now we know what happens in our brains and why. Although the context will vary, the process remains the same. *When you are consciously aware of a negative experience you expect to happen (a threat prediction), and what you actually experience does not match the prediction, your brain detects a mismatch between these two experiences. When the brain recognizes the mismatch, it unwires the neural network of the original pain-infused learning so that it can update itself with the new information. Moreover, the transformation is not just a surface-level change; it changes your brain at the synaptic level.*

By definition, implicit emotional learning takes place outside of our conscious awareness. Thus, as I discussed in Chapter Nine, it is not unusual for individuals to be surprised by the emotional learnings they unearth beneath their protective behavior. For many, simply recognizing and articulating the emotional learning that has been causing their problems creates the conditions for a spontaneous prediction correction experience.

I am not referring to the cognitive statement associated with the "That makes no sense" experience that accompanies this awareness frequently. As I mentioned in Chapter Five, that observation is the outcome of the thinking brain's assessment of the irrational logical nature of emotional learnings. However, when "That makes no sense" becomes a felt experience and not just an intellectual observation, it has all the makings of a prediction correction. It may be that just the felt awareness and recognition of the now-explicit emotional learning can be sufficient to unwire the synaptic wiring of an emotional learning and create a spontaneous 'Aha' moment when that awareness is accompanied by a felt experience of "That makes no sense."

Let me give you an example involving a client named Shandra. She identified a threat prediction that she could trace back to her early adolescence. It involved the threat of disappointing others, a common emotional learning that millions of us experience. However, this threat was not only affecting her career adversely. It was also taking a toll on her physical health. She decided to see me when her doctor told her she had to do something to reduce her stress.

She told me that for as long as she could remember, her parents used the silent treatment as a way to communicate their disappointment in her. There was no discussion or feedback, only silence. To protect herself from the pain of loss, rejection, and isolation she experienced, she developed an anxious hypervigilance. She monitored significant people for any signs of disappointment, such as loud sighs and a tight face with hard staring eyes or a cold silence. Now, at age 37, her body was registering the distress of her hypervigilance.

Although her threat prediction felt true, Shandra recognized a deeper truth:

"When I understood what was going on, it changed everything. I always felt that it was on me. I was the problem. I was carrying the burden of expectations, but they weren't my expectations. It was theirs for me. Today, I don't need to justify what I chose to do, as I have always felt I had to do. Just understanding where these feelings are coming from is freeing. Do I like it when my parents give me the silent treatment? No. But that is on them. They always come out of it as if nothing ever happened, while I continue to worry. No one except my parents has ever treated me that way; I just felt they would because that's what I learned. I can handle it if people are disappointed in me, just like I can handle my parents' silent treatment. I can even tell them that I'm okay if they are disappointed in me and hope they get over it soon."

By pairing the threat that caused her hypervigilance with her understanding of its origins and invalidity in her adult life, she was able to free herself from her past. She also recognized that talking to her parents about the effect their behavior had on her was unnecessary.

It can happen that once you discover and become aware of what your trigger is all about, and recognize that your brain is simply responding with a survival instinct based on something it learned in the past, you may have the same experience. One of the most effective ways to do that is by using Trigger-informed Mindfulness.

Trigger-informed Mindfulness

The practice of mindfulness has ancient roots in Buddhism and Hinduism. Its application in Western culture became mainstream in the late 20th century when Dr. Jon Kabat-Zinn developed a Mindfulness-Based Stress Reduction program. He merged modern science with ancient wisdom to help individuals manage the stresses of modern living.

Today, mindfulness-based practices encompass more than managing and reducing stress. Basic mindfulness awareness practices, which involve breathing, eating, meditating, listening, physical movement, and addiction recovery, are taught in various settings. Some might say that mindfulness is just another avoidance mechanism that has been overhyped and oversold. Maybe so. What I do know is that when we integrate the two key elements of mindfulness with the human technology for transformation that this book describes, the outcome is the foundation of *Living a Trigger-free Life*.

The two key elements of mindfulness practices are (1) becoming aware of and focusing on your present internal experience (thoughts, feelings, emotions, and physical sensations and (2) practicing a non-judgmental recognition and acceptance of that experience. Mindfulness is, by definition, non-counteractive!

Yes, this non-judgmental, non-counteractive approach can be challenging. However, this approach also supports the 5-step transformational process delineated in this book. **Let's review the 5-step process again with the added dimension of mindfulness.**

Step #1 – *Clarify the Problem Pattern and Your Desired Change*

Clarifying the problem and the desired change depends upon being aware of your real-time experiences, the behavior patterns that you want to eliminate, and the change that you desire. (Chapter Eight)

Step #2 – *Discover, Clarify, and Validate the Threat Prediction and Your Protective Behavior*

This step involves intentionally focusing on your internal experiences without judgment or preconceived notions and letting your emotions and feelings speak their emotional truth. The second part consists of being open and willing to identify your protective behaviors. (Chapter Nine)

Step #3 – *Test the emotional resonance of what you have identified and recorded by engaging in real-time observation of the threat prediction and its associated protective behaviors.*

Once again, a non-judgmental focus on internal experiences is essential to validating the emotional truth of what you have identified as the threat prediction. (Chapter Nine)

Step #4 – *Identify and Clarify the Threat Prediction Correction Information*

This step involves being attuned to your internal experience as you search for and identify experiences that contradict the threat prediction. Trigger-informed mindfulness also provides opportunities for spontaneous transformational experiences. (Chapter Ten)

Step #5 - *Make Your Brain Right by Making It Wrong*

Once again, we have an internal focus that juxtaposes the activated threat prediction with the prediction correction information.

Use the 5-hour window this pairing creates to intentionally update the old emotional learning with the correction information and other positive related information. Observe your experience and continue updating as needed. This step involves a dual-focus mindfulness approach. While the threat prediction is activated, you simultaneously bring the prediction correction into focus. You will be mindful and aware of both sets of information within you.

Trigger-informed mindfulness begins with the awareness that you want something to change in your life and clarifying the emotional learning that blocks you from experiencing that change. Rather than working to overcome or override your triggers or using techniques to soothe yourself after you are triggered, Trigger-informed Mindfulness uses these triggers as grist for the mill of becoming trigger-free and experiencing personal mastery and emotional well-being.

Four Ways to Make Your Brain Right by Making It Wrong

In addition to Trigger-informed Mindfulness, there are four other ways that you can make your brain right by making it wrong. (NOTE: If you are working with a therapist, they may also have other ways to create the mismatch experience.) The four I want to discuss describe what you can do on your own.

They all involve consciously and intentionally pairing a threat prediction with prediction correction information that contradicts that threat prediction. They are:

- The Two-hand process
- I feel this, but what I know is that my experiences tell me this
- Real-time discussion with those involved
- Emotional-time discussion with those involved.

The Two-hand Process - On One Hand, this ... and on the other, this ...

I have been using this Two-hand process for several years with my clients and know that several use it to facilitate their transformational work. It involves the following steps:

- Open your hands and intentionally focus on them. (It is a good idea to let them rest on your lap.) Select which hand will hold the threat prediction statement and imagine putting that statement and its associated feelings in that hand. Feel it in your hand. (Some of my clients hold that written statement in the selected hand).
- Read the statement as you focus on the hand holding that threat while you imagine or recall scenes in which that threat was activated. Feel the distress associated with it. Make the scenes as vivid as possible.
- Assess the degree of your emotional discomfort on an Emotional Pain scale of 1- 10, where 1 is calm and 10 is a high degree of discomfort.
- NOTE: It is essential to experience the feelings associated with the threat to activate the neural network in which it is embedded. This step does not unwire it; it primes it to receive the prediction correction information.
- After about 10-20 seconds, switch your attention to your other hand (the one holding the contradictory information). Read the prediction correction information. Maintain your attention on the hand holding that information, and let yourself become aware of what you have written and any feelings that arise within you .
- After about 10-20 seconds of focusing on the contradictory information, switch your attention back to your other hand (the one holding the threat prediction) and allow yourself to experience the threat again.
- After about 10-20 seconds, switch back to your other hand again and recall the contradictory information again.
- Continue the switching process for about 2-3 minutes, noticing the discrepancy between what the threat says and what the prediction correction says.
- After you have completed one set, notice any emotional shifts in your experience of the threat. Has the discomfort/anxiety associated with it decreased? (Use the scale of 1- 10 discussed above.)

Note:

1. It is not unusual to feel a sense of confusion and disorientation during this process.
2. Trust your brain and its adaptive and neuroplastic capacity.
3. Optimize the 5-hour window to continue the update process by recalling the prediction correction and related experiences as frequently and vividly as possible during that time.

You can repeat this process to help your brain unlearn what it learned that you didn't know it learned, and help it learn what you want it to learn based upon the truth of your experiences and understanding. After engaging in this process, I recommend that you observe how you respond in situations or interactions that usually trigger you.

I recommend that you also employ the Two-hand Process before you undertake any of the following interventions.

I Feel This, But What I Know Is That My Experiences Tell Me This

This protocol is similar to the Two-Hand Process, but it is enacted in real-time. It involves situations in which you are aware that (1) the threat prediction and the protective behavior are being triggered, and (2) you bring the prediction correction information into your awareness simultaneously. Think of it as doing the Two-hand process internally. You may recall how Janna, the 27-year-old nurse from Chapter Ten, and her hypervigilant need to have everything perfect experienced a real-time prediction correction. After she clarified the threat that caused her protective hypervigilance, she began to observe them being activated at work. After about a week of observation, she introduced a prediction correction to her brain when she became aware of how unnecessary her hypervigilance was in her present-day life.

As with all of the prediction correction interventions I present in this section, the essential step is intentionally pairing the felt activation of the threat with the prediction correction information. Thus, you are not counteracting or trying to overcome the feelings of the threat. You are engaging in observing and feeling it while simultaneously introducing your brain to the contradictory information.

This protocol often involves engaging in the behavior that your brain has been preventing you from doing and observing what happens. If you choose to do this, make sure you are aware of any expectations you have that others will change and the possibility that they will not meet your expectations. They have no idea what you are attempting to do (unless you tell them) and may react with their protective behaviors.

Real-time Discussion with Those Involved

Real-time discussions with those involved in the problem can be beneficial when you are prepared and are willing to take responsibility for the problem and your protective behavior. You will be experiencing the threat while you are discussing what you want to be different for yourself. Those involved may react defensively out of surprise or as a result of being activated themselves.

NOTE: I do not recommend using this intervention if the individual(s) involved are emotionally volatile, become emotionally dysregulated easily, have personality disorders, or can become abusive verbally or physically. Your freedom from the emotional tyranny of ancient pain-infused emotional learnings is not dependent on putting yourself in harm's way. You can use the next approach.

Emotional-Time Discussion with Those Involved

How many times have you imagined having a difficult discussion with someone? I'm referring to those inner conversations when we rehearse what we're going to say to someone and imagine their various responses, and then imagine the different ways we will respond depending on how we imagine they react. Have you ever noticed how much time and energy you spend on that rehearsal process and the anxiety it causes? (For example, think about my story about Mr. Nice Guy in Chapter One).

The focus of these kinds of interventions is on the other person(s) and preparing yourself to cope with their reactions. It is a communication process called other-referencing. In contrast, the Emotional-time Discussion is a self-referencing process. During this update process, you are imagining this discussion in emotional time. You will experience many of the feelings you would have if it were a real-time discussion because your emotional brain does not know time. Thus, this intervention can be effective when those involved aren't available, or it is not advisable to have a real-time discussion, as I discussed in the previous section. I want to illustrate how this works using Suzanne's story.

Suzanne Introduces the Prediction Correction to Her Brain

Recall that Suzanne described her trigger as a threatening feeling that meant this: *If I speak up and ask for what I want or use my voice to express my ideas or opinions, then people will shame and reject me like my father did. I will not matter to anyone and will be left alone without anyone to be with.* She also identified her protective behavior as *becoming anxious and withdrawing into silence or just going along with what is happening. I avoid telling people what I want and, if I can, avoid speaking up at work and sharing my ideas. If I have to do that at work, I will become anxious and worry that someone will call me out, and I will feel horrible shame. I must never express myself; it is just too dangerous.* She summarized her prediction correction as: *"Yeah, I learned that if I express myself and ask for what I want, people will shame and reject me, and I will then be all alone. I learned that long ago with my father when I didn't know what I was learning. The truth is, I have many experiences and memories of expressing myself and my opinions, and nothing bad has ever happened. I am creative and love to engage with people."*

Suzanne was equipped with the information that she needed to eliminate the original learning and the protective behaviors associated with it.

Illustration 11.2 – Suzanne Introduces Her Brain to the Prediction Correction Information

The numbers in the illustration correspond with the explanations below.

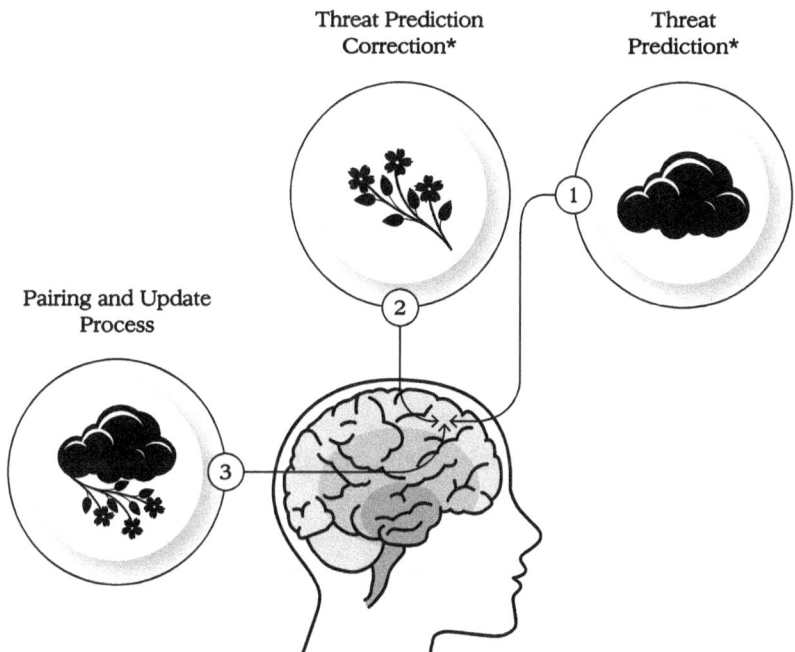

* *Threat Prediction*

If I speak up and ask for what I want or use my voice to express my ideas or opinions, then people will shame and reject me like my father did. I will not matter to anyone and will be left alone without anyone to be with. I must never express myself; it is just too dangerous.

* *Threat Prediction Correction*

Yeah, I learned that if I express myself and ask for what I want people will shame and reject me, and I will then be all alone. I learned that long ago with my father when I didn't know what 1 was learning. The truth is I have many experiences and memories of expressing myself and my opinions, and nothing bad has ever happened. I am creative and love to engage with people.

She first used the Two-Hand Process to initiate the transformation. She put the Threat Prediction in her left hand and recalled instances when she felt the threat. By doing so, she activated the trigger (the threat-infused emotional learning) and just let herself experience it for about 30 seconds. Then she turned her attention to the right hand and read the prediction correction that she had developed. She looked at the statement in the palm of her hand, recalling experiences of expressing herself and her awareness that nothing bad ever happened when she did so. She switched back and forth for about three minutes, as described in the protocol, and allowed herself to feel and acknowledge the difference between what she had learned and what she knew was her lived experience. This process paired the Threat Prediction with the Prediction Correction Information that she had identified, as depicted in Illustration 11.2.

1. Suzanne activates the emotional learning by recalling a situation in which it was triggered. She feels the anxiety and distress associated with the activated threat-infused emotional learning.
2. She brings the prediction correction information into her field of awareness to pair the threat prediction with the prediction correction.
3. Her brain recognizes the mismatch between what it learned and the new information. It unwires and opens up the neural network in which the pain-infused emotional learning is wired, allowing the learning to be updated.

For a moment, imagine with me what her brain might be telling her when it was presented with information that contradicted the emotional learning that she had acquired in her childhood. It might say something like this:

"Hey, what is going on? There's new information telling me what I learned isn't right! I know it felt right before, but now I know it is wrong based on this new information. I need to adapt myself to survive. So, I'll open up that old learning network and update it with this new information. That old learning doesn't apply anymore. I have to make sure I'm up-to-date so that I can make more accurate predictions and successfully adapt to the world around me."

Suzanne wanted to meet with her father and tell him about the harmful effects his behavior had on her. However, she considered two facts that influenced her decision not to do so. First, he was now a cranky, feeble old man. She also recognized that his behavior was simply a manifestation of an implicit emotional learning he had acquired in his childhood. There would be no benefit in discussing this with him. Second, she knew that she could 'talk' to him using the Emotional-time Discussion. She was already integrating the 'new Suzanne" into her life by practicing Trigger-informed Mindfulness to strengthen her transformation.

Suzanne also recognized that becoming trigger-free was going to be a journey for her. It was one that she gladly accepted. She might have described her awareness this way: *"I now have a choice I didn't have before. I can choose to express myself or not. I am no longer held hostage by the threat of being rejected and abandoned by my father."*

Now, let's take a look at the individuals in the nine examples we have been following since Chapter Eight to see how this last step plays out in practice.

Nine Examples of the Updating Process

This section describes the updating process of the nine client examples that we have been following in Chapters Eight through Ten. Each presents the desired change, the threat prediction, and the prediction correction, and describes the updating process. You may be sufficiently familiar with these stories now that you can jump to the Transformation and Update descriptions for each example.

I recommended that each of them use the Two-Hand Process to familiarize themselves with the pattern of thinking that forms the foundation of this update process. I want to repeat a message that it is an essential part of the paradigm shift that I discussed in the Introduction and throughout this book:

> *We have learned to overcome or counteract our emotional reactions and reactive behaviors. Thus, we have, for the most part, developed a pattern of thinking based upon counteracting the negative. The result is that nothing fundamentally changes. The 5-step process I describe in this book is based on doing the opposite. That does not mean embracing*

the negative. It means engaging with our problems and reactive behaviors to discover and clarify the underlying threat they protect us from experiencing. That way, we can transform them with a prediction correction. That is a very different pattern of thinking than most of us are used to. It is transformational!

With that in mind, let's now look at the nine individuals we have been following since Chapter Eight. I want to reiterate that each of them used the Two-hand process to familiarize themselves with the five steps of this human technology.

1. **Pauline**

    Desired Change:

    I want to be able to stay calm and curious with my friends and colleagues when they talk about their different experiences.

    Threat Prediction: *If people are talking about their activities and what they are doing as a family, I will be ignored and become invisible, just like what happened in Middle School when all the kids talked about their vacations and what their families were doing. I felt so left out that I just withdrew because I felt like I wasn't good enough. That all changed in high school because my mom started working. We had more money and did more things. That's when I started to feel like I had to jump in, just like today, or I would feel the same awful feelings I felt back then.*

    Prediction Correction:

    I know this feels true today, and the feeling of being left out and excluded felt true in middle school. But that was middle school. I remember many times over the past several years when I felt that anxiety and didn't jump in. I just let myself chill and listen to all the chatter. Folks often asked me what was happening in my life and how the kids were doing. I feel sad about what happened during middle school. If I could go back in time, I'd tell my younger self that we'll get through this rough patch and come out okay.

    Pauline's Update and Transformation Process

    Pauline had never done any formal therapy but had read several books about healing your inner child. When she became aware of the link between her present-day urge to jump in and the threat of feeling invisible and not good enough that she acquired in childhood, she used the Two-hand process to initiate the change she deeply desired. She also wrote a compassionate letter to her younger self. She told her younger self about what her adult self now knew she had learned about not being good enough and feeling like she didn't fit in, and how all that would change for her as she grew up. She used an Emotional-time Discussion to go back and visit her younger self and read that letter to her. In addition, Pauline incorporated Trigger-informed Mindfulness into her life.

2. **Simone**

Desired Change:

I have imagined myself talking with Jeremy about how depressed and tired I feel, and that I need him to step up and even recommend counseling for us. I want to make that image a reality and have the conversation that I keep avoiding. It is the conversation I know my mother never had with my dad, and it took a big toll on her.

Threat Prediction:

If I speak up for myself and bring up what I am feeling and my feelings of frustration and the weight of carrying Jeremy's happiness, then I will cause him great hurt, and I feel like he will disappear into a puddle of helplessness, and it will be my fault. Then I will be stuck with him, helpless, and my kids hating me.

Prediction Correction:

The biggest threat to me is that my kids hate me for hurting him. But will they really hate me? That is way too big for me to answer. What I do know is that I hate myself and feel like I am breaking down. I know I will survive the stress of talking with Jim when I tell him about my concerns for him, myself, and our marriage. All these years, I have never said a word. Just had to be the quiet, good wife who supports her husband. Even if the kids hate me, at least they will have a mother who isn't depressed and having to pretend she is okay. I can work it out with them.

Simone's Update and Transformation Process:

Simone recognized an intergenerational rule for women in her extended family: You don't talk about problems with your husband and maintain harmony. Just swallow your feelings and keep marching forward like a good wife. She also knew her two cousins both suffered from depression and unsatisfying marriages. She chose to use two approaches to move forward. One involved the 'Two-hand Pairing Process,' and the other was to have a real-time discussion with Jeremy about what she had uncovered and the change she wanted for herself and their marriage. However, before doing that, she imagined having a conversation with both the living and deceased women in her extended family. She described it as her declaration of freedom and a responsibility she felt to her daughter to break the pattern. As she put it to me, *"I don't want my daughter to inherit the obligation that I did, and the only way to do that is to talk about it and put it where it belongs, in the past."* (NOTE: Simone did have the essential discussion with Jeremy, and he agreed to do couples counseling. However, after several months of weekly couple sessions, Simone informed me that she had decided to file for divorce. It was just too much work taking care of him and also being there for the kids. She did inform me that her children were both seeing a therapist who was helping them through the transition and was also involving her and Jeremy in some of the sessions.)

3. **Gary**

    Desired Change:

    I want to trust that I can be in a stable, close relationship in which I feel I can be open and caring without feeling like I am never doing anything right because I never know what right is or it is always changing.

    Threat Prediction:

    If I get too close to someone and start to care for them and let them care for me, the other shoe will always drop, and they will switch on me and reject me. It will be just like it was at home with my mother. I was either her favorite, or she ignored me like I didn't matter. I never knew which mother would show up. I know how to survive ups and downs, but stability is unpredictable and actually scary.

Prediction Correction:

My mother had a serious mental problem, which my father and her family ignored. When I look at my relationships, I see how I need to create chaos for myself because I learned how to survive chaos. Knowing that stability is threatening feels strangely true, and it is also freeing. I recall two significant relationships that felt easy and open and went well until I started to get anxious, and now I know why. I have developed many friendships that feel stable and supportive of me. And even when things get a little rocky because of miscommunication, they have never rejected me.

Gary's Update and Transformation Process:

Gary used the Two-hands process to contrast his identified threat prediction with the correction. Gary continued in therapy for about six months after discovering and updating the threat of being in a stable relationship. During that time, he met with his father and discussed what he had learned about his capacity to be in stable relationships and how he had changed. Although his father found it difficult to understand what Gary told him, he did comment that he had to ignore his mother's behavior because bringing it up caused her to get very angry and sometimes threaten suicide.

4. **Nancy**

Desired Change:

It is important to me that I stop pretending when I am with my family. I want to tell my mother that I see the world differently from her and that it is okay for her and me to be that way. I want to let her know I love her and that it makes me sad that she sees the world that way.

Threat Prediction:

If I don't go along with everybody, pretending everything is okay, they will accuse me of being selfish and hurting mom. They will be angry at me and turn their backs on me. I must play the game of pretending.

Prediction Correction:

I know mom had a tough childhood and moved in with her sister's family when she was five. From what little she has talked about, the rules were strict, and the punishment harsh. It was a big Catholic family with nine kids. Now that I know about emotional learning, I imagine she learned things about surviving that I can't imagine. No wonder she sees the world the way she sees it. But I don't have to take her sadness and pessimism home with me after visiting. I don't want to hurt mom, but I can tell her that I see the world differently and still love her. If my family is upset with that, I can ask her if it is okay for me to see the world differently from her. I know she will say yes, and even if she doesn't, I can still affirm that I love her. My family isn't going to turn their backs on me because I see the world differently from them, and if they do, I have the communication skills to deal with it. After all, it is my story that they will do that, and I have no basis to believe it other than I somehow learned to feel that.

Nancy's Update and Transformation Process:

Family relationships can be challenging, especially when threats of ostracism and blame feel real. Nancy wanted to avoid causing problems for her mother while freeing herself from the tyranny of the pretend game. After several rounds of the Two-hand Process, she decided to have a real-time discussion with her mother during her next visit. She reported to me that the discussion helped her mother open up about her childhood and how she didn't know that her attitude about life had such an impact on Nancy. Nancy told me. *"My mother told me she thought that everybody in her family saw the world like she did and was glad to hear that I have a different attitude"*.

5. **Leo**

Desired Change:

I want to be free of the anxiety and threat of being judged for doing something wrong. If I make a mistake, I want to know and feel that I will be okay and can deal with it.

Threat Prediction:

If I am judged and found guilty of doing something wrong, I will be punished by being ignored and sent into exile, where I will be all alone. I must not be found guilty of doing something wrong, so I must always do things perfectly or find a way to please people so they won't find me guilty.

Prediction Correction:

When I look back, I can see where this comes from. We all had to act like the perfect family. From our clothes to our grades, from church services every Sunday to how we ate our food, there was no room for error. And when we did slip up, we'd always get the look, especially from dad. I thought I had left all that behind when I moved away. But when I remember the look today, I can feel myself being judged and found guilty. But nothing ever happened. I was never exiled or even sent to my room. I know I can handle not being perfect now that I'm in my thirties. It was different for that little guy back then. How could he have known that not being perfect is normal and human? Yeah, I'm not perfect, and I'm not guilty of not being perfect, and I'm not alone. I'm okay, just like that little guy I was back then was okay."

Leo's Update and Transformation Process:

Leo used the 'Two-hand Pairing Process' to introduce his brain to the correction and 'Trigger-informed Mindfulness' to continue the update process with one simple statement, *"Yeah, I'm not perfect, and I'm not guilty of not being perfect, and I'm not alone. I'm okay, just like that little guy back then was okay."*

6. **Manny**

Desired Change:

I want to be able to talk with my adult children about how I feel and discuss my concerns about how they feel. I know they know how their mom felt trapped by her mother, and I don't want them to feel the same way.

Threat Prediction:

If I talk about what I want in my relationships with Jackson and Jacqui, I feel they will feel I need them to take care of me. I will then be a burden like my mother-in-law, Mary, was for many years to my wife, Sue. They will then be angry at me for being so dependent on them, as she felt. I will not let them be angry with me for trapping them like Sue was by her mother.

Prediction Correction:

I'm not my mother-in-law. I am very independent and have a circle of folks I enjoy being with. Sue never had that because Mary sucked all her time and energy. I can talk with Jackson and Jacqui and share my concerns and observations. They are not going to be angry with me for wanting to spend more time with them and their families, and I know they will discuss it. I just never realized that what was causing me so much concern was my story that I would be like my mother-in-law was to Sue, a burden that drained the life out of her.

Manny's Update and Transformation Process:

When Manny became aware of the threat prediction that was causing him so much distress, he was surprised that his brain had learned he would be a burden to his adult children, just like his mother-in-law was to his wife. He knew he could free himself from worry and discuss his desires with them. Before talking with Jackson and Jacqui about his 'story', he used the Two-hand Pairing Process.

7. **William**

Desired Change:

The only change I want is to be able to tell people what I can and can't do when they ask. I want to negotiate different responsibilities with my boss and set some limits with my wife.

Threat Prediction:

If I don't do what important people in my life ask me to do, they will blame me for their unhappiness, and it will be my fault that their lives will be ruined. I know this sounds ridiculous, and I know it's not true, but it feels so true. I must do what I am asked to do, or else I will suffer the pain of disappointing my family, my parents, and my boss. They will then leave me and never come back.

Prediction Correction:

I am proud that I am a dependable and responsible person whom others can rely on. My wife isn't going to cut me out of her life if I explain all this to her. She might even be happy to hear that I am finally acknowledging my own needs, instead of always worrying about others and trying to please them. I am aware that my boss is aware of and values my abilities, and we will be able to explore ways for me to better manage the demands of my position.

William's Update and Transformation Process:

When William identified the threat prediction that drove his anxiety-driven behavior, he experienced a spontaneous transformational experience in session. He described it like this: *"It feels like I've been in some kinda trance or something and I'm just coming out of it. Where have I been? This is so weird to feel. I get it, and I know I can talk about this with Geri and also with my boss."* Before his conversations with them, he used the Two-hands process to update the threat prediction with the truth of his experience and his recognition of "waking up". In addition, he integrated Trigger-informed Mindfulness into his everyday interactions with his family, friends, and at work.

8. **Cyrus**

Desired Change: *I want to slow down and hire a manager-type person who can do the running around I have to do. The business can afford it, and I can handle the books, but the daily grind is getting to me. That's hard to admit because I have always worked a lot.*

Threat Prediction:

If I slow down and take some time to relax, I will be judged as lazy and will be in trouble. Punishment always follows. I will be attacked with cruel words and could even be beaten up for not working like I am supposed to. This is what happened with my father, especially when he was drunk and angry.

Prediction Correction:

My father is dead now, and he can't hurt me anymore. I know that. But I didn't know that his words and his beatings were still affecting me so much. Now I know that I have worked hard so that I wouldn't be punished. It feels strange to know that, but it makes sense and feels right. I built a good life for my family. I can slow down and relax, maybe even take a long vacation with my wife. The past is over, and I am free to, as my son tells me, just chill.

Cyrus' Update and Transformation Process:

For most of his life, Cyrus has been suffering from big "T"rauma due to the emotional and physical abuse inflicted by his father.

Several sessions of EMDR helped him with some of the symptoms. He also had an emotional-time discussion with his father to inform him that he would no longer carry the burden of his sad and unhappy life. It is interesting to note that Cyrus kept his prediction correction statement with him and read it whenever he started to feel what he called the threat of boredom. He acknowledged that it was not an easy transition for him as he explored other interests besides running his business.

(NOTE: Much to my surprise, Cyrus left me a message about 18 months after our therapeutic relationship ended. He was at a Yoga retreat with his wife in Mexico.)

9. **Sally**

Desired Change:

I want to be clear, direct, and respectful in my communication and relationships with my team members. I also want to calmly follow up with them on my requests.

Threat Prediction:

If I am clear, direct, and even respectful in my communication with my team members, they will see me as a bully who doesn't care about their feelings. Then they will leave me, and my practice will fail, and I will fail. As I think about this threat, I can feel it. But I also see where I learned this. The rule in my family was to never ask for what you want because anybody who did was criticized for acting like they were more important than anybody else and accused of being a demanding brat who didn't care for others.

Prediction Correction:

This is my practice, and I am a thoughtful, conscientious dentist who has the best interests of my patients and team in mind. But I have been ignoring my best interests for fear of breaking family rules and being labeled a bully. It is interesting to me that many team members keep asking me for more direction, and I have also been ignoring their requests. And when I have provided that, they have always acknowledged it. I will meet with them individually and take responsibility for being indirect in my communication. I will tell them I know it has been challenging for them to know what I want because I haven't communicated it clearly. I am not and never have been a bully.

Sally's Update and Transformation Process:

After completing several rounds of the Two-Hands Process, Sally chose two approaches to changing how she communicated with her team. The first one involved a team discussion in which she would take responsibility and apologize for not being clear in communicating her expectations regarding protocols and patient communication. The second approach was to hold individual monthly meetings with each member to review their experience with her clear and direct communication, ask for suggestions on how it could be improved, and follow up on her requested changes. Sally recognized she was changing the culture of her practice, and it would take time and commitment to make that transition happen.

Now It Is Your Turn

I recommend starting with the Two-hand Process and observing what that experience is like. Depending upon your circumstances, you may also choose one of the other update processes. As many others have, you may find that simply being aware of the threat using Trigger-informed Mindfulness can provide opportunities for a spontaneous update and transformation.

An old idiom says that "the proof is in the pudding". In terms of the human technology for transformation I have described, that means that your lived experiences will provide the opportunities to assess its effectiveness. Some clients have found that the threat level associated with a specific emotional learning is significantly reduced, while others observe a gradual internal shift. Most of my clients report that simply being aware of what is going on when they are triggered has created an internal sense of control and mastery that they had not experienced before.

Summary

This chapter presented the fifth step in the five-step human technology process designed to help individuals update pain-infused emotional learnings acquired unconsciously in the past. These emotional learnings feel true and no longer apply to adult life. However, they continue to trigger suffering and protective behaviors.

The core message of "**make your brain right by making it wrong**" is that by intentionally pairing these outdated emotional learnings with corrective information, you can achieve enduring emotional transformation and freedom from triggers.

Experiencing Life after Transformation

In Chapter Two, I discussed how Derrick's wife experienced his transformation. After several attempts to change his withdrawal pattern, he told me that he felt different and that Marie was experiencing that difference as well. The withdrawal-push away pattern that they had developed over the years had shifted. Derrick was having a different experience with Marie, and she was also feeling a shift within herself that was uncomfortable for her. It may seem strange that while Derrick was giving her the attentive listening she wanted, Marie was uncomfortable. However, when patterns shift in relationships, even when they are beneficial, it can be uncomfortable and disorienting.

This pattern-shifting process and its emotional influence on others are seldom discussed in self-help publications. However, it is essential that you are aware of it and know how to manage it.

In Part III, we will discuss the shifts that this human technology can create in your relationships with others and how to manage the effects of those shifts. In addition, I would like to extend one more invitation to you and ask you to join many others who are choosing to walk a path less traveled.

Chapter Twelve
Pattern Shifts:

Navigating the "This Is a New Experience for Me and Others"

Do you recall the last time you went through a transition? It may have involved a new job, a move to a new city, the end of a significant relationship, or the birth of a child. Experiences of a transition are often marked by a bit of confusion and disorientation as you (and your brain) become accustomed to the new environment or situation.

This is the experience that many of my clients have had as an outcome of applying the five steps I have described in this book. It is not uncommon for me to hear statements such as, *"This is different. It's new for me."*

In Chapters Eight through Eleven, you learned how to update old problem-generating emotional learnings. Your transformation will inevitably shift the dynamics of your relationships, affecting others emotionally and behaviorally. This chapter explores this neglected topic. There are three topic areas we will discuss:

1. The **emotional and behavioral effects of the pattern shifts** that your transformation will create in your relationships;
2. The **sense of disorientation** that often accompanies the powerful transformations generated by this 5-step human technology;
3. The importance of **strengthening your new experiences and using specific communication skills** to assist you when others comment on their own new experiences of you.

Let's begin by discussing what it was like for Suzanne as she began to express herself and what she wanted in her personal and work relationships.

Suzanne and Her New Experience

Although Suzanne recognized that her inner work to be trigger-free was not complete, she also acknowledged that her distressing emotional reactions had subsided considerably. She was experiencing the change that she desired: *to express myself and my thoughts and preferences, recognize that people may not always agree with me, and know that they have the same freedom I do.* Rather than freezing up behind the inner wall of protection when she was triggered, Suzanne felt a slight inner quiver, like a thin curtain moving in a light breeze. She used that feeling as a signal to remember her prediction correction information and continue her transformation to becoming trigger-free.

Now, she could express herself and what she wanted, what she was interested in, and her ideas at work. For the first time in her memory, Suzanne felt like she had a voice. It was not just a different experience for her; it was a new one.

In addition, it was also a new experience for others. They were all familiar with and had grown accustomed to Suzanne's pattern of quiet withdrawal. Although her friends acknowledged and liked her expressiveness, they were unfamiliar with the "new Suzanne." Her manager in particular was a bit thrown off by her openness, and her boyfriend told her that while he liked the new Suzanne, he had to get used to her.

They all may have been happy to see the change, but for them, it meant a shift in their relationship with her as well. They and Suzanne were experiencing a natural phase inherent in all transformational shifts and transitions: patterns were shifting, and pattern shifts nearly always involve some discomfort for those affected by the change.

Pattern Shifts

Imagine holding a six-piece mobile in front of you. Now, imagine pulling down on one of the pieces. The outcome is obvious; all of the pieces must shift. The balanced pattern that existed before you pulled one piece has changed. If you let go, it will move back to its former pattern. The point is that when one piece of a system, such as a mobile or a relationship, shifts, all of the other pieces shift with it. I use this simple illustration to discuss what happens when we change the patterns that we use to relate and communicate with others.

Throughout this book, I have emphasized that patterns are inherent in how we live, work, play, communicate, and relate. Although I have not found any specific research on the percentages, it is estimated that automatic learned and instinctual behavior patterns account for up to 90% of our behavior. In comparison, intentional behaviors account for the remaining 10%.

In Chapter Three, I discussed how we often use idioms to describe emotional experiences that feel ominous, threatening, or foreboding and for which we have no words. Many refer to shifting the balance within an emotional system, such as a family, the workplace, or personal relationships, with phrases such as "Don't rock the boat", "Don't upset the apple cart", and "Don't make waves." These, and many like them, communicate one rule: Don't make anyone uncomfortable by doing something that upsets the patterns that we all use to protect ourselves from emotional discomfort.

Patterns of behavior exist in every relationship in which you are involved. Although the degree of significance varies—relationships with close friends, intimate partners, or family members are usually more significant than casual friendships—patterns are inherent within all natural systems, human and otherwise.

Thus, what do you think happens to the mobiles of your relationships when you become less reactive, more open, more present, more expressive, more assertive, and more focused? Your internal transformation manifests in how you relate, communicate, and live—and that influences others. Sometimes, those shifts can be uncomfortable for others, and they may try unconsciously to make you return to your old behavior patterns so that they don't feel the discomfort of your shift. Let me shed more light on this seldom-discussed topic.

During my hospital administration career, I worked as the Administrator of an alcohol and drug abuse treatment center. One of the things that made the center unique was the family treatment program that it had developed. This was in the early 1980s, when treatment programs began to recognize that both the individual and the entire family needed treatment. The members of the family mobile had developed patterns of pushing away and withdrawing from the source of their distress, the addicted family member. With treatment, the system's patterns would shift; thus, not only was the 'identified' patient treated, but the family system also needed help to adjust to the change.

I bring this to your attention because you may be rocking the boat, making waves, or upsetting the apple cart as you transform the way that you relate, communicate, and behave. As beneficial as your changes will be for you, others around you may experience them at both a conscious behavioral level and an unconscious emotional level. They, like you, may become somewhat disoriented by the pattern shifts. It's essential to be aware of this.

Some may be uncomfortable and not know how to tell you that they are, or they may use a protective behavior to avoid doing so. Others may be appreciative and glad. Just be mindful that as you transform yourself and make the changes that you desire, others will have to adapt to their new experience of you. As liberating and wonderful as becoming trigger-free can be, it can also be confusing to others.

The Experience of Disorientation

For new patterns to emerge, old patterns must disintegrate. The space between the disintegration of the old and the emergence of the new is often a time of disorientation. That is what happens whenever we start doing something with which we are unfamiliar: we have few patterns with which to orient ourselves.

We often experience this after the death of a loved one, a divorce, the birth of a child, a new job, a move to a new location, or other major life events. Families whose homes are destroyed by tornadoes, hurricanes, or fires, or have been robbed, will experience it intensely. It is an emotional state often marked by confusion, anxiety, doubt, and uncertainty. Sometimes, it can lead to situational depression. However, we can also experience it when we make the kinds of transformative changes this book discusses.

Very few self-help books discuss this stage of the transformation process. When you make the deep, life-altering, and life-giving changes you can make with this 5-step process, you will see and experience the world differently. However, you will be aware that the world has not changed. The difference in your perception of the world will be a unique and subjective experience, and your sense of disorientation may be minimal. Yet, it will be there, and it's another sign of the profound transformative change you have made.

However, as I alluded to in the section above about pattern shifts, those around you and those with whom you work and have personal relationships will also experience some degree of disorientation in their relationship with you. After all, they're used to you acting one way, and now you're behaving differently. As subtle as these changes can be, you are changing your brain intentionally. New patterns are being created, and old ones are disintegrating. This provides opportunities to reinforce the transformation and own the difference.

Owning the Difference

It may seem strange that the people around you are a bit uncomfortable and even confused with their new experience of you, just as you may be by your new experience of yourself. If that happens, it is a sign that a transformation has truly occurred. Here are some responses I suggest that you consider if people begin to tell you about the change that they are experiencing in your behavior. This is about owning and reinforcing the difference in yourself that you are experiencing.

You Seem Different

If anyone remarks that you seem different, I encourage you to own the difference and ask them what the difference is like for them. Acknowledge that you have been working on changing certain behaviors. You can even be specific about the changes you are making. For example, Suzanne did this with her manager when he commented on her expressiveness in meetings: *"Yes, you've told me in the past that you'd like to see me express my thoughts and ideas more. I've been working on that, and your feedback tells me it's working. Thank you."* Every time you own the difference, you strengthen it.

You Seem Different, but I'm Not Sure What the Difference Is

If someone comments that you seem different, but are unsure what the difference is, thank them for being so observant. Then ask them if they'd like to know what changes you have been working on. If they say yes—and most people will—tell them about the changes you have been making. This helps to confirm and affirm the change that you have made.

I Don't Know What to Expect Anymore

If you receive feedback from family members or others that they feel a little uncomfortable being around you, as if they don't know what to expect anymore, treat that as a great sign. It means that you have changed. You can tell them that you, like them, are still getting used to your changes and that you are glad that they recognize them. Take every opportunity to acknowledge and affirm your changes and strengthen the new.

Strengthening the New

When clients tell me that they feel different, I first want to support and encourage them to build on their new experiences. Returning to the quote I used at the end of the Introduction, you are no longer fighting the old but building the new. Here's a suggestion that can help you with that.

Go back to the **statement of your desired change and write it in the present tense**. For example, Suzanne's original statement was: "*I want to express myself and my thoughts and preferences, recognize that people may not always agree with me, and know that they have the same freedom I do*". She rewrote it in the present tense: "*I express myself and my thoughts and preferences, recognize that people may not always agree with me, and know that they have the same freedom I do.*" It reads like an affirmation. However, recall that Hebb's Axiom tells us that neurons that fire together wire together. Thus, every time Suzanne recalls experiences of expressing herself and recalls that statement, she strengthens the wiring. What might have been a fruitless affirmation has now become a **reinforcing confirmation**.

Two Important Communication Skills

Although the experience of change will be internal, you will know it by observing yourself in relationship with others and within the context of your life. That change will also be evident externally in the way you relate, communicate, and behave. That is the change that people will see and typically comment on. As a result, I recommend two communication skills that I believe will be beneficial to you. Although these skills are nothing particularly new, they are often neglected or forgotten.

Use the Pronoun "I"

Have you ever noticed how often individuals use the word 'you' or 'we' when they are talking about themselves and their thoughts, observations, or experiences, instead of the word "I"? If you haven't noticed it, take about a week to observe it. You will see it happening with newscasters, friends, family members, and coworkers. There seems to be an aversion to the word "I". Maybe it's because we can hide behind 'we' or 'you', or it's a cultural norm that has developed over time. I don't know the reason. I suggest trying "I" when you mean "I" and notice your subsequent experiences.

Be Curious

The second communication skill is curiosity. When I discuss curiosity, I'm not referring to using the word 'why'. You may know by now that the word 'why' is not particularly effective when you are asking people about their thoughts, opinions, or behavior, and can generate a protective behavior in the person to whom the question is directed.

However, curiosity is one of the most powerful communication skills that we can use. I suggest the use of simple curious phrases such as: "Tell me more?", "I'm curious about your thoughts about... (whatever subject), or 'What is that like for you?" As discussed in the section about disorientation, curious questions are beneficial when people ask you about or comment on the changes that they are experiencing in their relationship with you.

Application in Intimate Relationships

Although it takes two to Tango, it only takes one to initiate the dance! I say this to let you know that you can work on improving your intimate relationship by applying this transformative process for yourself.

In this chapter, I used the mobile metaphor to illustrate how one individual's transformation of their protective behaviors shifts the balance of the entire relationship. In human mobiles, this shift is often experienced as uncomfortable. When you make a shift, those around you will see and feel the difference. They have to make some adjustments. If you choose to integrate this human technology into your personal and intimate relationships, I suggest the following six guidelines:

1. You want to have a different experience of yourself in your relationship and have clarified what that difference is (Steps One and Two). You are also clear with yourself that the change you want to make does not mean changing your partner.

2. You have clarified the pain-infused emotional learning that, when triggered, activates your protective behavior, what that protective behavior is, and how that emotion is triggered in your relationship (Step Three).

3. You are willing to be open about what detrimental effects you think your protective behavior is having on the relationship.

4. You are willing to ask your partner's permission to discuss how you want to behave differently in the relationship, and the learned emotional reaction that is interfering with that experience.

5. You are willing to inform your partner that you are seeking to update problem-generating emotional reactions to improve and strengthen the relationship (Steps Four and Five).

6. You are willing to:
   - Take complete responsibility for the behavior pattern that you want to change.
   - Acknowledge that this change may cause some emotional discomfort for you and your partner.
   - Be open to listening to and respecting your partner's feedback and experience.

Summary

Chapter Twelve addressed the natural consequences of personal transformation within relationships. It highlighted how shifts in your behavior and emotional responses create new experiences for both yourself and others, potentially leading to temporary discomfort or disorientation.

The chapter also emphasized the value of acknowledging and communicating openly about these changes, offering practical strategies to reinforce your transformation. By owning your differences, strengthening new behaviors, and utilizing mindful communication, you can effectively navigate relational shifts, reinforcing your path toward personal empowerment and emotional well-being.

When the Rubber Hits the Road

You have probably heard the phrase 'When the rubber hits the road' numerous times in your life. It refers to the instances when a plan, idea, or theory is put into practice in real-world conditions and situations. The rubber of this 5-step human technology hits the road when you are interacting in the world of relationships. After all, we learn the three Rs of Rules, Roles, and Relating in our relationships, and thus, it is in our relationships that we can update them.

Our relationships provide the catalyst for transformation. Choosing to live a trigger-free life entails our choice to update the pain-infused emotional learnings that get in the way of the life, love, and success we desire. It is a choice to walk a path less traveled.

Chapter Thirteen
Choosing a Path Less Travelled

I would like to share one of the most fulfilling experiences I have had as a psychotherapist since I began using the neuroscience-based human technology for transformation presented in this book. That experience involves feelings of gratitude, appreciation, competence, and curiosity. I feel:

- *Grateful to the neuroscience researchers who discovered memory reconsolidation and the pioneering psychotherapists who applied that research in practice.*
- *Appreciative of my clients who are willing to walk a path less traveled.*
- *A sense of competence that invites me to learn and grow in my profession.*
- *Curious about what will happen within the psychotherapy profession as this neuroscience-based paradigm shift for helping others becomes more mainstream.*

As I write this final chapter, I find myself wondering what you are thinking about the information that I have presented. I am curious about any insights that you may have had about your triggers and how you may be integrating a different way of thinking about human behavior and the world around you, just as I have been doing since late 2015. I hope I have communicated the paradigm shift in understanding human behavior that it represents.

I am also reflecting on a statement attributed to Albert Einstein: *"The significant problems we have created cannot be solved at the same level of thinking that created them."*

Although he was a physicist, I don't think he was referring to physics; I suggest that he was referring to the significant problems that human behavior causes. We are stuck in a frustrating, fruitless, and fracturing cycle of trying to change our problematic behavior by overcoming it rather than addressing its causes. The outcome is a surface change that changes nothing, or as an 1848 French epigram put it, *Plus ça change, plus c'est la même chose,* meaning the more things change, the more they remain the same.

I am sharing these thoughts with you because the inner work that this book invites you to do can be daunting. I have provided many recommendations that I believe will help make it less so. However, it can be challenging to:

- *Allow yourself to feel what you have learned not to feel—and what your brain doesn't want you to feel.*
- *Discover past unconscious emotional learnings and bring them into your conscious awareness, even if you are working with a therapist who understands emotional learning and the new neuroscience of memory reconsolidation.*
- *Recognize when your thinking brain causes you to question, and sometimes dismiss, what you discover about what your emotional brain learned that you didn't know it did.*
- *Stay with the feeling and meaning of an emotional learning that feels true, even when you know it isn't.*
- *Let your emotional brain speak its truth so that you can update it with the real truth.*

You will experience internal questions and resistance that will distract you. I say all of this based upon my experience applying these five steps in my life and with my clients.

However, let me add this. A strong sense and experience of personal empowerment emerge from and accompany this hard work. It is an inner knowing and a solid self-awareness that you can:

- *Eliminate distressing emotional reactions and strengthen your emotional resilience and well-being.*
- *Free yourself from the tyranny of problem-causing emotional learnings that you didn't know that you acquired.*
- *Enhance your physical and mental well-being.*

- *Deepen your capacity to experience greater joy, delight, happiness, and good old fun.*
- *Increase the positive influence you have on others.*
- *Solidify your self-respect and respect for others.*
- *Apply a human technology to optimize our brain's evolutionary survival bias so you can thrive and prosper.*

One of my clients recently shared his experience of applying the five-step human technology for transformation presented in this book. I am grateful for his willingness to share that experience with you. I could not have said it any better.

> *"It's like I now have something tangible I can think about and change instead of going into a spiral of frustration, self-criticism, and self-doubt. I have a way of understanding and thinking about my problems and the obstacles within me by using that sentence you gave me, "If this, then this, and then thinking, what about this?" I am experiencing a growing sense of self-confidence and inner strength, which I am still getting used to. And you know, what you can see in yourself, you can see in others. I can see their reactions are their protective behaviors, and that the real person lives beneath them."*

No Unique Problems, But Very Unique Solutions

This book included many of my clients' stories; you may have identified with one or more of them. My intention in doing so was to provide you with examples of applying this five-step process. You have probably also noticed that, although the nature of the problems varied from person to person, the essential issues they reported could be categorized into three main types: pushing away, pulling away, and avoidance. These protective behaviors take an enormous physical, emotional, and mental toll on us. They also prevent us from fulfilling our deep desires to thrive and experience the love, success, and joy that, I believe, is our birthright.

I am bringing this to your attention because you may have a similar experience to my clients: while the nature of the problem, such as specific situations that involve certain people and your life experiences, will be unique to you, the protective behavior that you exhibit when you are triggered will not be. Our species has used the same protective behaviors for hundreds of thousands of years. *However, your prediction corrections will always be unique to you.*

As you shed the light of your awareness on the problem-causing threat-predicting triggers that you identify and work to eliminate, you will learn how to identify the essential ingredients of prediction corrections. You may see where or when your unique threat predictions caused you difficulty. You will be walking the less-traveled path of discarding and updating pain-infused emotional learnings that no longer serve you, and learning new ways of experiencing yourself. If you choose to walk that path (and I hope you do), you will learn to trust yourself, this human technology for transformation, and an Inner Feeling Voice that quietly beckons you to be all that you can be, your Authentic Self.

The Invitation Revisited

If you read a book about how to write a self-help book, it will recommend that the final chapter serve as a call to action. It will offer inspiration, encouragement, and the promise of a different and better future. I want this last chapter to do that for you by revisiting the invitation in the Introduction—to become trigger-free and experience personal empowerment and emotional well-being. It is "Choosing a Path Less Travelled."

I sincerely appreciate your consideration of that invitation. I hope this book has given you the knowledge, encouragement, and inspiration to accept it. I am sure that you have surmised by reading this book that becoming trigger-free is not a matter of reprogramming your subconscious, positive thinking, or overcoming obstacles. It involves intention and attention combined with a solid willingness to take responsibility for one's life and one's reactions to life as it presents itself.

If you accept the invitation, I believe you are choosing to:

- *Participate consciously in evolution.*
- *Relinquish a threatening past that we keep remembering and recreating.*
- *Create a future that makes us worthy of being called Homo sapiens, the wise ones.*
- *Walk the path of a Homo leornian, a learning one, a path less traveled.*

Ultimately, you are choosing to say "I".

To Say "I"

I end this book with a poem. I do not know who the author is and have been unable to find out. Thank you to whoever you are. Your words have been a source of hope, inspiration, motivation, and courage for me and countless others.

I want to say I
    to say I
    and mean it
But that's an awesome act.

To say I is to
    take responsibility for
        my thoughts
        my actions
        my attitudes

my feelings
But that's an awesome act.

To say I is to
    choose an identity
    accept a name and a face
    cease being an it
    be willing to be known
    be accountable for my life
    respond to life
    open myself to the response of others
    eliminate the possibility of hiding
    end the practice of blaming others
But that's an awesome act.

To say I
    is to be me,
    all of me.
    I want to...
But that's an awesome act!

I wish you peace, joy, wonder, success, and happiness as you choose a path less traveled.

Appendix

Section #1 - The Five-Step Human Technology for Enduring Transformation

Section #2 - The SFT (See-Feel-Think) Protocol for Strengthening Memories of Positive Experiences

Section #1

A Template for the 5-Step Human Technology for Living a Trigger-free Life

Step #1 - Clarify the problem pattern and your desired change

The problem I have is ...

Desired change – The change I want for myself is ...

Step #2 - Discover and clarify the threat prediction and the protective behavior you use to protect yourself from the predicted threat

If this ... then this ....

To protect myself from the pain that my brain predicts will happen if I make the change I desire, I must ....

Step #3 - Observe and validate the threat prediction and protective behavior.

Observing the threat prediction and its related protective behavior helps to validate it and make revisions if needed.

Step #4 - Identify and clarify the threat prediction correction information.

Identify experiences or create experiences that contradict the predicted threat.

However, ...
But, ...
What about this ...

Step #5 - Make your brain right by making it wrong by pairing the threat prediction with the prediction correction information.

Look for and/or create opportunities to disconfirm the threat prediction by pairing the threat prediction with the prediction correction information.

Section #2

The See - Feel – Think (SFT) Approach to Strengthening Memories of Positive Experiences

SEE - How do I see myself in the theater of my mind?

FEEL - How do I experience myself emotionally as I see myself having this positive experience?

THINK - What positive thoughts, beliefs, or stories do I have about myself as I let myself remember this positive experience?

Personal example:

I'm out with friends, enjoying the laughter and sharing that we're all engaging in.

I see myself talking and engaging with my friends. I feel open and connected to them and am enjoying the feeling of belonging. I am worthy of the joy and fun I am experiencing. I belong.

Work example:

I had a good day at work as I completed several projects and also got some high-fives from my coworkers. I see myself focused and present. I like the feeling of being grounded, knowing I can handle challenges. I am good at what I do, and I enjoy the feeling of being capable.

Resources

www.emdr.org

www.emdria.org

www.traumahealing.org

www.aedpinstitute.org

www.coherencetherapy.org

www.istdpinstitute.org

www.ifs-institute.com

References

Barrett, L. F. (2018). *How emotions are made: The secret life of the brain.* London, UK: Pan Books.

Cozolino, L. (2002). *The neuroscience of psychotherapy: Building and rebuilding the human brain.* New York, NY: W. W. Norton & Company.

Csikszentmihalyi, M. (1990). *Flow: The psychology of optimal experience.* New York, NY: HarperCollins Publishers.

Damasio, A. R. (1999). *The feeling of what happens: Body and emotions in the making of consciousness.* New York, NY: Harcourt Brace & Company.

DesRoches, B. (1990). *Reclaiming Your Self.* New York. Bantam, Doubleday, Dell.

Ecker, B. (2015). Memory reconsolidation: Understood and misunderstood. *International Journal of Neuropsychotherapy, 3*(1), 2–46. https://doi.org/10.12744/ijnpt.2015.0002-0046

Kegan, R., & Lahey, L. L. (2009). *Immunity to change: How to overcome it and unlock potential in yourself and your organization.* Boston, MA: Harvard Business School Publishing.

Pally, R. (2008, June 28). The predicting brain: Unconscious repetition, conscious reflection, and therapeutic change. *Psychoanalytic Review.* https://doi.org/10.1516/B328-8P54-2870-P703

Rilke, R. M. (1934). *Letters to a young poet.* New York, NY: W. W. Norton & Company.

Schacter, D. L. (1996). *Searching for memory: The brain, the mind, and the past.* New York, NY: Basic Books.

Schutz, W. (1994). *The human element: Productivity, self-esteem, and the bottom line.* San Francisco, CA: Jossey-Bass.

Siegel, D. J. (1999). *The developing mind: How relationships and the brain interact to shape who we are.* New York, NY: Guilford Press.

Bibliography

Damasio, A. R. (1994). *Descartes' error: Emotion, reason, and the human brain.* New York, NY: Putnam.

DesRoches, B. (1995). *Your boss is not your mother: Creating autonomy, respect, and success at work.* New York, NY: William Morrow.

DesRoches, B. (1991).

Doidge, N. (2007). *The brain that changes itself.* New York, NY: Viking Penguin.

Ecker, B., Ticic, R., & Hulley, L. (2012). *Unlocking the emotional brain: Eliminating symptoms at their roots using memory reconsolidation.* New York, NY: Routledge.

Engel, S. (1999). *Context is everything: The nature of memory.* New York, NY: W. H. Freeman & Company.

Espinosa, L., Bonsall, M. B., Becker, N., Holmes, E. A., & Olsson, A. (2022). Individual differences in affective learning predict intrusive memories. *Behaviour Research and Therapy, 157,* 104161. https://doi.org/10.1016/j.brat.2022.104161

Fogel, A. (2009). *Body sense: The science and practice of embodied self-awareness.* New York, NY: W. W. Norton & Company.

Izard, C. E. (1991). *The psychology of emotions.* New York, NY: Plenum Press.

Jung, C. G. (1913). *The theory of psychoanalysis.* London, UK: Forgotten Books. (Reprint 2018)

Lane, R. D., Ryan, L., Nadel, L., & Greenberg, L. (2015). Memory reconsolidation, emotional arousal, and the process of change in psychotherapy: New insights from brain science. *Behavioral and Brain Sciences, 38*, E1. https://doi.org/10.1017/S0140525X14000041

LeDoux, J. (1996). *The emotional brain: The mysterious underpinnings of emotional life.* New York, NY: Simon & Schuster.

Panksepp, J. (1998). *Affective neuroscience: The foundations of human and animal emotions.* New York, NY: Oxford University Press.

Rossi, E. (1993). *The psychobiology of mind-body healing.* New York, NY: W. W. Norton & Company.

Watzlawick, P., Beavin, J. H., & Jackson, D. D. (1966). *Pragmatics of human communication.* New York, NY: W. W. Norton & Company.

Meet The Author

Brian DesRoches, MHA, MSC, MBA, PhD, LMFT

Brian DesRoches, PhD, has been in private practice as an experientially-focused psychotherapist since the late 1980s. While practicing psychotherapy, he has also provided coaching, consulting, and workshop facilitation for the dental profession. His approach to these services integrates practical applications of 21st-century neuroscience with proven interventions to enable individuals to develop both internal resources and external skills, ultimately experiencing personal mastery, emotional resilience, and overall well-being.

Before transitioning to psychotherapy and coaching, he was a hospital administrator and vice president of a multi-hospital corporation. Brian has an extensive professional education with a Master of Health Care Administration, Master of Science in Counseling, Master of Business Administration, and Doctorate in Pastoral Counseling and Psychology. He has been trained in several therapeutic modalities such as EMDR, Brainspotting, Internal Family Systems, and Coherence Therapy, and has taken advanced courses in therapeutic applications of modern neuroscience.

Brian is the author of *Your Boss is Not Your Mother* (William Morrow, Inc., April 1995; also published in 6 foreign languages) and *Reclaiming Yourself* (Dell Publishing Inc., April 1990). He also developed and facilitates workshops for the dental profession, focusing on Practice Leadership, Developing the Extraordinary Team, and Optimizing the Six Skills of Patient Communication.